LETTERS FROM WANDERLUST

A ONCE-IN-A-LIFETIME SPIRITUAL ADVENTURE

around the world, on one-way tickets

HECTOR JESUS ARENCIBIA

ISBN: 978-1-4834-4909-8 (sc)
ISBN: 978-1-4834-4908-1 (e)

Lulu Publishing Services rev. date: 03/30/2016

"When you are comfortable on your path,
it doesn't matter where it leads."

—Abraham

I dedicate this book to those of you who are in the pitfalls of the internal night. It is my intention that it serves as the bringer of your dawn. May it shepherd you toward the light.

PREFACE

Letters from Wanderlust

The most difficult task I set out to accomplish while writing this book was how I could pen a very personal story and do so in a way that would allow it to be a life rejuvenating and soul nurturing piece of literature for you the reader. Then, one day, as most answers to the perplexing things in life are received, it dawned upon me. Ironically it happened right before the book was completed. The revelation was like this: "Let the audience know that the story is not entirely about your journey or you. Yes there are magical places beyond the comprehension of imagination visited, and so too are there very personal core rattling experiences shared, however advise your readers to leaf through the pages for the undying principles tightly woven in the fabric of this life adventure. Let the book serve for what it was intended; a source of inspiration, an activator of spiritual remembrance, a transmitter of timeless divine truths. It must be egoless for it to flourish. You are solely the messenger." And as you will soon discover, a most unlikely messenger I am.

I never imagined my life journeying through the spiritual path but that is the beauty of Spirit: It has the power to touch and lift us all. No matter how unorthodox our choices in life are.

It is said that before the break of dawn, the fervor of darkness is at its most potent and I couldn't agree more:

My name is Hector Jesus Arencibia and I am 35 years old. By the time anyone comes across these words I could be at least 36 years of age if not much older. I was born and raised in Miami, Florida. I am a first generation American. Sandwiched between two beautiful sisters, I am the only son of dual Cuban immigrants. I grew up in a financially volatile household. Some years we were living above middle-class standards. During these years my parents would throw me and my siblings over-the-top birthday parties with designer cakes that were decadently stacked higher than our tiny bodies. These lavish events also included scores of clowns, the best caterers in the city, and overstuffed piñatas. Our Christmases were even more extravagant, with gifts from "Santa Claus" that included a motorcycle for me when I was merely eight. Other years we were very close to dirt poor and collected food stamps in order to be able to eat. My parents divorced while I was at a very young age. Splitting my time between homes is how I remember most of my childhood and adolescent years.

Just as the monetary and parental stability in my life was inconsistent, so was my religious upbringing. Throughout most of my youth we considered ourselves Catholics, however I never did my Communion and we never went to church other than to attend weddings. When I was ten my mother converted into some sort of extreme Christianity. I still hold on to a few specific memories of this time. Like the one where the members of the church entered our home one day and pillaged it of all Catholic relics. One act entailed the smashing of a white ceramic Virgin Mary that had "blessed" our garden for as long as we'd lived there. Another episode had a full-on drum circle in the living room that served to cheer on a woman who was speaking in tongues while intermittently delivering messages from "The Heavens" to everyone present. I believe this phase of extreme Christianity lasted a couple of seasons. After that, my mother never really found another connection with organized religion again, but she always held on to her faith in a Higher Power. On the other hand my father was never a religious or spiritual man, as far as I could tell.

As a teenager I always found myself more interested in what the older kids were doing. By the time I was in the eleventh grade most of my friends were already out of high school doing grown-up things. I emulated them by puffing on Newport cigarettes, and slinging back fruit punch colored cocktails at shanty nightclubs with very loose door policies. At nineteen I transplanted myself to New York City to fulfill my childhood dream of living in the Big Apple. That experience greatly assisted in defining who I am now. In being away from all the influences of home, and exposing myself to the pandemonium of NYC, I first discovered my love affair with writing. In moments of solitude and insanity, I found company and serenity in the space between a pen and a piece of paper. Throughout my time in the "concrete jungle" I supported my dream of big city living by working random jobs. I was once even a chipper greeter for the Windows on the World Restaurant located on the 107th floor in Tower 1 of what was once the World Trade Center. I graduated from the Borough of Manhattan Community College with an associate's degree in liberal arts.

After almost half a decade of living in NYC I grew tired of the hectic life, frigid winters, and the perpetual loneliness that came from living away from home and family. So at twenty-four I packed the small number of things I owned and headed back down south to sunny Miami. The next ten years ushered in my downfall into addiction. Unfortunately, I chose a highly popular lifestyle in South Florida that glorifies drugs and alcohol. It was common to be offered cocaine at a party or in a nightclub several times in an evening. I easily got caught up in the falsehood this way of living encourages, which is the more bottles you pop and the more cocaine you hoover, the more likeable you become — and I became very "likeable".

By the time I was 34 my addiction had sabotaged three loving relationships. Blacking out during a night on the town became the norm, and disturbingly, I found that funny. I even thought it was cool. Many mornings I would wake up not knowing how I made it home — if I was even at home. I developed this philosophy that if I didn't remember what happened the night before then it didn't matter, it did not happen. I abused alcohol almost on a daily basis and experimented with other drugs as well. I began to have more contact with my drug dealers than with my own family and friends. Eventually thoughts of suicide began to incessantly haunt my mind. I found myself in the darkest of days where the only way out seemed to be through death's door. I also was suffering from panic attacks and insomnia. My daily escape from this nightmare was to wash my tears and fears down with alcohol, or better yet chase them away with my newfound drug of choice: Ketamine.

Ketamine, known as "Special K" or just "K" on the streets, is primarily a veterinary medicine. It is an injectable sedative for animals that is legally distributed in liquid form in small viles to veterinarians. Drug users take Special K out of its vile and dump it onto a plate or pan, which is then placed in a microwave or conventional oven for heating. When the liquid is exposed to heat it solidifies and turns into a flaky white powder. Once fully cooked this scaly powder must be compressed. It has to be turned into its purest powdery form so the user can sniff it. A typical user will compress Special K by dicing it repeatedly with a credit a card on the same plate or pan it was cooked on until all the flakes have become a fine powder. Not exactly a simple process, and as you can see I was an expert at it.

I was enamored with this drug because it disconnected me from reality, taking my mind to another realm where I would be present but I could not feel any emotions. Pain and suffering did not have any power over me, they could not enter my mind, after all the drug is a sedative. Special K is not cheap and my daily use had gotten to the point where the average transaction with my dealer was priced at about three hundred dollars. I was quickly burning through all the cash I had earned from several successful real estate deals. In short, I had become a public alcoholic and cocaine user who was always ready for a party. I was the epitome of the rock star Miami lifestyle. Privately, I was elbow deep in sorrow. I'd become a bank account plundering tragic mess, and a borderline suicidal, Special K abuser. My life was a continual cataclysmic event.

December 26, 2011 changed my life. It was the day I had my first awakening moment — although I didn't know it then. I struggled to get up that morning after spending the previous night, which was Christmas, abusing as usual. After managing to get out of bed I felt an overwhelming urge to go look at myself in a mirror. At first I resisted, then finally gave in and drug my sorry self over to the chunky framed floor-to-ceiling mirror in my living room. As I stood there something I can't explain came over me. While staring at my sad visage, I said to my reflection, "What the fuck am I doing with my life?" I ordered myself: "You can't continue to do this." In the next moment the image of my face transformed: It looked like I'd been badly injured in an accident. A violent panic attack erupted, I couldn't take it—I had to close my eyes and turn away. Everything was somehow becoming clear to me. I was overcome by a sense of infinite wisdom, telling me that if I continued on this path of abusive behavior I would end up badly injuring or killing myself; or even worse hurting other innocent people.

I knew I needed to act fast. However I also knew that I was not capable of fighting off these demons alone. I went to the solemn place where I've always found my only spiritual inspiration: my grandfather's grave site. Even though he passed while I was only four and I do not have any recollection of him, I've always had a strong connection to his presence, and I've always gone to his grave whenever I've been in serious need of spiritual help. An hour later, sitting next to his grave, I reverently spoke to him: "Grandpa, help me get out of this mess. Please send me light, and since I can't promise *myself* that I'll stop this drug abuse and drinking, I make this promise to *you* that I will stop. But please, please, please help me."

The following day I had a flight to Vienna, Austria where I'd begin a three week holiday that consisted of traveling through other cities including Budapest, Prague, and lastly Berlin. Upon arrival to Vienna I felt a disarming sensation of warmth in my chest. The feeling can only be compared to that when you're in love, except it was even warmer, stronger, more powerful. Wherever I went and wherever I was, everything felt absolutely sublime. My mind no longer entertained thoughts of suicide. I could look into everyone's eyes more profoundly, seeing them for who they really were, the vessels to a beautiful soul. When my vacation was nearing the end I was afraid that this newfound rapture would also come to a screeching halt.

To my surprise this feeling of astounding joy only grew stronger upon my return home. Miami, the city where I was born and raised, the city I'd lived close to 30 years, appeared absolutely brand new to my eyes. I roamed the streets at all hours in pure ecstasy. I was so in love with everything that even the garbage cans seemed absolutely beautiful to me. It had slipped my mind that I'd asked for light and clarity at my grandfather's tomb a few weeks back, and I believed that this constant feeling of love and happiness had come from my travels. So I began to investigate the possibility of taking a trip around the world.

Even though I didn't know precisely where I was going or how I was going to get there, I sold off most of my worldly possessions, both to symbolically free me from attachment to material things, and to help me finance the trip. First to go was my dining table. It was probably worth two thousand dollars but I sold it for five hundred. Then my entire living room set, my bedroom set, my iMac, and even clothing items. This was a period of total uncertainty but the one thing I was sure of was that my life was changing, that I was going to leave it all behind, and set out to see the world. I was acting as if it was already going to happen, when technically I did not have the financial means to do so. I was working the law of attraction. I then broke my lease and shacked up in an empty place where I knew I could stay rent free, and joyously slept on an air mattress.

Shortly after the move I received a message from an old partner in my real estate business notifying me that mutual clients of ours, Barry and Tom, a gay couple from NYC, were interested in selling their current property and buying a new one. After a few days of Barry and Tom's apartment being on the market it went under contract for sale. The contract was solid, it was an all cash deal scheduled to close in less than sixty days, offering close to the asking price. Confident that their current property would close Barry and Tom signed a contract to purchase a new home. The money I needed for my trip around the world was manifesting right before my eyes in the shape of the commissions earned when both deals closed.

The transactions took three months to complete. During that time I became engrossed in reading spiritual books such as *The Tibetan Book of*

Living and Dying (twice), *Many Lives Many Masters, The Bhagavad Gita, Warrior of the Light,* and *The Power of Now* (three times). It was while reading the preface of *The Power of Now* where Eckhart Tolle describes his spiritual awakening experience where it finally hit me that I too was encountering a divine uprising from within, and that this journey I was embarking upon was the result.

On May 4, 2012 with nothing more than a couple of ideas in my mind as to where I wanted to go, a few obtained visas, $16,500 in my bank account, and an agenda that consisted of going wherever my heart desired, I strapped on a backpack, bought a one-way ticket to Los Angeles and boarded the plane. At that moment the only thing I knew was that this journey was in the hands of The Divine and I was going to let it guide me.

From here on out, this book will unfold in the style of a diary. It will include pictures of the places that inspired my writings, insights, and life lessons. I will take you along on a very personal, transformational, and profound four-month pilgrimage that lead me to 21 countries on five of the six habitable continents.

CHAPTER 1

Banking on Faith

(My Pre-Journey Insights)

E very action that lead me through this journey was an act of faith. It felt like ten thousand alarm clocks had simultaneously gone off in my soul and because of this I believed it to be my destiny. During the three months prior to my embarking, these spiritual clocks would go off at all hours of the night waking me with the profound urge to write. The Divine called and I answered. What follows in this chapter are the writings that transpired from that very magical and fecund period of deep awakening.

January 27, 2012 – Miami, FL USA

The most astounding journey you will ever take in your life starts internally. The instant you allow yourself to accept, trust and connect with that universal greatness that lies within, your life begins to change. Once you are connected there is not a single thing in existence that can stop this eternal well of good from overflowing inside of you, because it comes from an omnipotent and universal place that is infinite in its existence.

February 3, 2012

Dispel disbelief by doubting doubt itself. Speak your truth loudly, clearly, and very often. Receive an outpouring of immeasurable rewards by becoming a modern day messiah.

February 5, 2012

We're all but the "forty-niners" of the spiritual Gold Rush, and our job is to lay the foundation for the megacities of the future. Turning sleepy villages into boom towns, we're the founders of The Divine uprising that is now occurring on Planet Earth. Together we will catapult human consciousness unfathomably forward.

February 6, 2012

The moon is the earth's disco ball. Every night without fail she hovers over the planet and provides us with the quintessential glow for us to live, love, laugh, kiss, converse, paint, make music, dance, get to know each other a little more, and do as we freely will, without ever charging us a penny. This evening look up at the sky, find the moon, give her a nod or a wink, and say "thank you" as an acknowledgement of your indebtedness.

FEBRUARY 9, 2012

The universe is designed to ceaselessly aide and nurture us, to receive its help all one must do is hold an unwavering belief that this is true. Then we must allow ourselves to openly receive all of life's joys that come from this inexhaustible well of prosperity and abundance.

FEBRUARY 10, 2012

When we free our minds of worries and "what ifs" we become limitless in our possibilities. Because the only limitations a healthy, human being living a privileged lifestyle has are the ones he or she places inside their mind.

FEBRUARY 11, 2012

The second you accept your own mortality as an inevitable process of life you will begin to live with more vigor, more passion, and most important of all, you will show more love and compassion for all things in existence. Since today we lost an un-duplicable celestial voice that went by the name of Whitney Houston, I say, let this loss remind us that our life on this planet is temporary — so why not live and love a lot more and make your stay and those of the ones around you the best it can possibly be.

FEBRUARY 14, 2012

To all the soldiers of light and love, let us use our weapons of goodwill and ambassadorship to make a difference in someone else's life for Valentine's Day. Today is all about love, and well, love has no limits on who or what it is intended for, so go ahead, do a good deed, hug strangers, plant a tree, reconnect with old friends, call your mother, surprise someone with something nice. This is your duty!

February 15, 2012

It has become entirely clear to me that I must broadcast this message of light with the force of a 10.0 love quake and that I must use every single tool I have at my disposal to do so. I am not afraid to speak of it and run with it, for it is my calling.

To do a great thing one must think a great thought and carry it with an even greater conviction.

February 18, 2012

Having recently looked at my entire life being put in storage and just clearing my Indian and Australian visas, it is slowly dawning upon me that my backpacking journey around the world is rapidly becoming a reality. Within just a few short weeks I will begin to trek across possibly 5 continents on a quest for something deeper than I have ever known. This is not a vacation, this is a true pilgrimage. I am not doing this just for self-fulfillment. What I want out of this journey is to inspire, lift and push people to go out and courageously reach for everything they want in life. I want people to know that anything they dream of they can attain, if they believe in themselves enough.

February 26, 2012

In observing a plastic world where not getting the right temperature or enough whipped cream in one's coffee is considered an actual problem and even cause for irritation, I'm left to wonder how far we have strayed from love, and how distorted the illusion of life has become for an alarming amount of people. Many of us don't like when it rains, yet that's what propels the cycle of life. Others complain about the sun ("It's too damn hot today!") yet without it, Earth couldn't be. Sadly the only goals of the citizens in this plastic world I am observing are to own more and more crap to fill the void they keep making deeper by enslaving themselves to the system that brainwashes them to think that acquiring material things will bring them happiness. I know firsthand because I was once the mayor of this plastic world, and I am immeasurably grateful that I was given the wisdom to move out and head over to the tiny village of organic living and independent thought.

FEBRUARY 28, 2012

Imagination is the catalyst to all things that are real. Anything that has ever been created by man was first imagined: Hot air balloons, space ships, the wheel, the Internet, the telephone, electricity, and absolutely everything around you. With this said, don't ever let anyone stop or belittle your imagination (your dreams), because nothing and I repeat, nothing is impossible.

Our ultimate responsibility as temporary occupants of this planet is to leave it in a better state than it was when we first arrived. If we remember this every day we will spread more joy, more love, more color, more music, more light, more life, more peace— and less and less of things that ultimately do not matter.

MARCH 14, 2012

Take a leap of faith, move away, start from scratch, run a marathon, climb a mountain, jump out of a plane, talk in front of a big group of people, ride a giant roller coaster, go to faraway places, and be scared till you're just not scared anymore, relinquish fear at all costs. For that is what it means to be alive.

MARCH 23, 2012

There is a certain indescribable magic in continued positive thinking, writing, speaking and acting. It's almost like putting on an invisible cloak to negativity: you just don't see it and it doesn't see you; you are not affected by it.

MARCH 24, 2012

Tonight I attended a dinner party orchestrated by a dear friend of mine, "Dr. Gerry". It wasn't a regular supper gathering where the guests sit at a long horizontal table, have parallel conversations with each other, say a few polite words to their tentative neighbors, and leave. This event was headlined with a golden ticket after the feast: the opportunity for a psychic reading held privately in a bedroom tucked away from the dining area. The chance encounter was with a very well-known clairvoyant whose specialty is in reading the Akashic Records (seeing into past lives). Everyone present was transfixed by this opportune evening. The energy in the air was palaple. Excitement tingled on my skin as if it had been freshly palmed by a feminine hand. The dishes poured out from the kitchen, and the more ebullient the party of 8 became. The sooner the meals withered off our plates, the quicker our one-on-one sessions with the life reader would begin.

By the time the first dessert bowl skidded across the table, the announcement was made: "It's time to start the show." I'm not entirely sure who went up first and why but after three guests returned from their psychic readings, I studied their reactions, and noticed they were all polarized. One woman, bordering 40, sat at the far end of the table with her face awash in tears. The second, a younger man in his late twenties acted like a monk who'd taken a vow of silence, gazing into his untouched dessert plate as if he was hypnotically watching television. I wondered what he was ruminating. The third, another middle-aged female could not contain her nervous chatter about all the good news she was just given. It was finally my turn.

For days upon end, leading to this moment, I was intrigued beyond imagination about this encounter. The marquee in my mind was aflutter with thoughts of what she might say. There I was, a few weeks away from setting sail on one of the most important journeys a man can take during

6

his life, and I was given this auspicious chance by an old friend who had recently "popped" right back into my life after years of being absent. I was doubtless that this moment was indeed guided by the hands of The Divine, and this very instant was the opportunity to let it speak to me through this fortune teller.

I walked into the room and was surprised by the banality. No crystal balls or religious statutes were present, just a soft-spoken, redheaded woman plainly dressed in dark blue jeans, and a tightly knit chunky sweater. I had never seen her before in my life. She sat behind a teeny round table draped in a soft white cloth holding a thick deck of worn-out tarot cards in her ghostly colored hands. Her energy was pure and despite her frail body, her "presence" was grandiose. I eagerly drew out the chair in front of her and took a seat.

A fraction of a second later, her eyes were shut, and she burst into prayer using a euphonious voice with a hum reminiscent of when one rubs a wet finger on the rim of a wine glass. She simultaneously shuffled the deck of cards in her hands. After a few chants she reopened her eyes, and asked me to grab half of the deck so that it would be split in two. I did as I was told, and my now divided fortune was strewn out on the colorless cloth.

As the last card was set into place her eyes burst wide open, but offered a blank stare. Already in a trance, she put her index finger in the air with her right hand and used the left one to make a spinning gesture around her index finger (as if she was turning an invisible basketball). She channeled the following: "You're going to take a trip around the world very soon. This journey you're embarking on is to reconnect with the energy of lands lived on in past lives. Your soul must revisit its old haunts in order to bring it closure for the havoc it wreaked during other lifetimes. On these travels, you will intuitively listen to your heart, and let it guide you, as it will take you exactly where you must go. Revelations will manifest. Once you have cleaned up your karmic disorder, your gifts will be revealed. You will uncover your destiny."

I was paralyzed in truth. I found the strength to nod my head as if I was being deeply lectured on something I had complete knowledge and agreement on, yet I had never heard any of it before. This abrupt change in my life was starting to make a lot more sense on a very profound level.

MARCH 27, 2012

In the pursuit of happiness one must be relentless.

MARCH 30, 2012

The reason why some of us never reach a truly content state in life is because we are seeking happiness outside of ourselves. The biggest mistake we make is to think that we will find it in another person, with another job, having more money, or even owning nicer clothes. We fail to realize that all these things are impermanent: the clothes will fade, possibly rip and definitely go out of style. The money will come and go just as most people will. What will never cease to exist is all the beauty and love that is within us. So let's nurture it, honor it, love it, respect it, and enthrone it by recognizing it is all we will ever need.

APRIL 7, 2012

Now more than ever, we are at the brink of a pivotal shift in human consciousness. We are rapidly moving toward lighter and higher frequencies. Every day I am personally witnessing awakenings from strangers on the street, and even close friends to not-so-close friends. It's almost like an alarm clock is going off inside all of us. We are beginning to understand that we cannot survive as a race if we continue to live in the current state of fear, lack, depression, hate, and anxiety. Instead, we are beginning to know that we can live a life filled with joy, love, and compassion — and it is a choice we all can make.

April 16, 2012

Become a ceaseless believer in magic and miracles, an endless dreamer who basks in the golden rays of the sun even amidst the most turbulent weather. Be an unshakeable mountain of faith whose peak cannot be reached or measured. Always remain calm.

April 17, 2012

"A coward is incapable of exhibiting love, it is the prerogative of the brave." - Mahatma Gandhi

All I have ever known and believed in has been love. I can't hold back and act like it doesn't exist in order to please others. I refuse to tread lightly on this issue while others stomp on their soap boxes complaining, preaching hate, division, and bigotry. However foolish it may sound today I make a further commitment to firmly stand my ground on this belief. I will continue to amplify my voice louder and louder in the name of love and light.

April 23, 2012

Don't be the rabbit that chases the carrot held at the end of the stick that can never be reached. If you are going to work, make sure you do it out of passion and love. Ensure that your every waking moment is fueled by your hearts desires. If not, you will have wasted your entire life chasing a dream that was never yours to begin with. Think about it. As a kid, did you dream about cashing a check or retirement benefits? Did you see yourself working a job you hate for 300 days a year to look forward to a mere 10 to 20 days off? It's never too late to tap into your childhood dreams and change the course of your life. Remember who you were then and what you fantasized doing as an adult. Do not give up on him or her. Dream, believe, become.

April 27, 2012

Despite all the excitement I feel for the journey ahead of me, there is also a deep sense of melancholy. Although the months and maybe years ahead may turn out to be the best I will have ever lived, knowing that I am walking away from absolutely everything and everyone in my life is a very bittersweet feeling at this moment. My last Friday night in Miami begins now.

April 28, 2012

Small, faithless minds will live small and faithless lives. They will spend their living years like a hamster on a wheel, endlessly running yet going nowhere — accomplishing absolutely nothing.

April 30, 2012

Never let your thoughts or dreams get warped by the opinions of small minds. Stay on your path of ambition at all times, no matter what others may say or think, for it was these same type of small thinkers that believed the earth was flat, that we could never fly a plane, or much less venture into outer space.

May 3, 2012

The hours are winding down. I don't know when or if I'll return. I've never been so clear in what I'm doing despite it being the biggest and riskiest thing I have done in my life so far. I sense it's a stepping stone to what's to come, and that's all I have, a sense, but that's all I need. A chapter in my life ends today and a new one begins tomorrow. I have no fear. I bank on faith.

CHAPTER 2

The Point of No Return

Everything that I needed to do in order to put my home life on a complete hold was done. I was most certain that I'd taken care of everything, but just in case I didn't, I bought myself some mental insurance by holding on to the thought that if I'd forgotten something, then it probably wouldn't be important while I was away. Strapped with just a backpack, a one-way ticket from Miami to Los Angeles in my hand, and a second one-way ticket from L.A. to Nadi, Fiji already purchased, the journey of a lifetime begins now.

MAY 4, 2012 – FT. LAUDERDALE AIRPORT

I am filled with a profound sense of wonder, and dumbfounded with absolute and endless joy.

There is beauty in everything I see and touch. I find myself looking deeply into people's eyes and instantly making a connection with their souls. I've realized what truly matters, and that is to love and be in love with every moment. I must share this wisdom with the world. It is my duty.

MAY 7, 2012 - LOS ANGELES, CALIFORNIA

There is an estimated 24,906 miles around the earth. Subtract the 2,348 miles that I traveled from Miami to Los Angeles, and it leaves me with 22,558 miles to go. Within a few short hours I'll board a plane and fly 5,550 miles to the Fiji Islands. I'll quickly gain some momentum in miles traveled leaving me with 17,008 miles to go. The very moment I land in Fiji I'll no longer have cell phone service, and will be limited to sending my smoke signals via whatever Wifi is available on my journey. This dream is really manifesting and if there's one message that I have for anybody who is reading this, it is the following:

Believe in your dreams. Surround yourself with positive people who'll lift and encourage you to go further in life. Think and speak like the person you want to be, starting from now. Ensure that your motives in life are fueled by passion and love, and not money! Believe in a Source higher than yourself and tap into it daily. Whether it be through prayer, meditation, yoga, dancing, etc., there's no wrong way to connect to the Source. As long as it feels true to your heart, keep doing it. Don't let the opinions of others alter what you fundamentally believe in your heart. Never doubt yourself and the power you have to accomplish anything.

Take time to relax. You are not your job, nor are you a social status, a color, a race, a creed, or anything that society would have you believe. You are infinitely more!

The fulfillment of your aspirations may take time but never lose heart or renounce your effort.

The denial of small meaningless pleasures will lead to the manifestation of largely significant happenings.

PACIFIC PARK – SANTA MONICA, CA USA

This was my first time visiting the Golden State. I'm pretty sure that the crisp warmth emanating from the rays of the California sun balanced by the cool of the Pacific Ocean is what inspired the song *California Dreamin* by The Mamas & The Papas. With sublime weather, coupled with the enchantment of the Santa Monica Pier, I was inspired to have my first photo of the journey taken. In my right hand I am holding the little black leather book I was already using to write down the names and collect signatures from the people who will cross my path on my adventure. My arms are wide open as I am embracing all the magic that is occurring in and around me. It feels great to be alive!

May 11, 2012 - The Fiji Islands

It's 3 AM Saturday morning in Nadi, Fiji. I just woke up. My body is still on L.A. time and thinks its 8 AM Friday morning. Crossing the International Date Line and being in a remote, lush and tropical island in the middle of the Pacific Ocean is teaching me firsthand that the earth is one strangely huge and magnificent place filled with endless wonder... I never dreamt it would feel this big and I've only seen a small fraction of it. I am humbled.

Here I am amidst drunken and aimless travelers, adventure seekers in mud bathed hiking boots, a small army of Swiss volunteer workers who've come to teach at a local school, ukulele toting dread-head stoners, Fiji natives sporting flat top afros draped in floral print garbs, blonde bikini clad Nordic volleyball players, gypsy cab drivers who will gladly overcharge you given the chance (I know, I already got jacked and quickly learned about them, I guess it's my fault for not listening to the hostel staff), a loquacious Canadian girl who has just arrived from China, wannabe surfers in body suits waxing their boards and practicing their "moves" on the gravel, a rotund and feverish Scottish man (who blames his illness on the mosquitoes and will happily show you his wounds one-by-one, pointing to all the bite marks over his sweaty body). It's 11:07 AM on a Saturday morning. Welcome to the un-photographable experience that is The Fiji Islands.

May 12, 2012 - Port Denarau Marina

The port to living a life of magic is always open to anyone who is willing to believe it is there.

There is something in the Fiji Islands that sparkles with more brilliance than its crystalline beaches. It is the effervescent heart and soul of its people. On every corner you are greeted with the word "Bula" which means hello. At times you may also get a handshake paired with a "Bula" from the men, and it's not uncommon to be invited into a stranger's home or an unassuming shop and asked to partake in a Kava ceremony.

A Kava ceremony is a welcoming, and during it you must remove your shoes and sit in a circle, around a black bowl. While attending a ceremony, in a humble shop, the owner told me that bowl represents how Fijians see themselves: united as one. They are all part of the same source. The bowl is then filled with a mixture of powdered Kava root (Kava is a native plant to the islands) and water by the head of the household or shop. Next, a prayer is said, and those in attendance must clap three times before anyone is offered a drink of the concoction. The first to have a drink is the guest, who is encouraged to share a life story, thus quickly bonding him or her to the hosts.

Looking out from the backseat of a taxi cab today, I noticed a group of children, no older than eight and no younger than five, playing with branches, throwing peace signs up in the air at me. T-khan, the driver of the cab, had just recently lost everything he owned in a cyclone that flooded his town with eight feet of water. He and his wife spent 36 grueling hours on the roof of their dilapidating home waiting to be rescued. Despite what he went through, you could see that his inner happiness was intact. You'd think that nothing had ever happened to him, and that is because Fijians make the best of everything. They tell you to relax and take your time, because after all you are on "Fiji time". I am certain that these philosophies for easy living are what make the faces of the natives radiate with so much warmth, and why laughter comes so effortlessly here despite a highly visible economic hardship. I have learned several invaluable life lessons from the people of the Fiji Islands and I am forever indebted. "Vinaka Fiji" (Thank you Fiji)!

SABETO MUDSPRINGS – NADI, VITI LEVU, FIJI

I could not help but to put my arms around the girls at the mud springs. They were so generously kind and engaging I felt as if we'd been friends for a lifetime. The girl on my left is Salote Tupo. She lives in a tiny village not too far away from the baths and suggested I post this picture on my Facebook timeline. The last thing I would've imagined that day was that I'd be told by a native Fijian working in a remote mud springs to post a picture onto my Facebook profile. Social media is literally everywhere!

May 14, 2012 – on flight FJ911 from Nadi, Fiji to Sydney, Australia

- Giving up alcohol and drugs was the best thing I could have done with my life.
- The foundation of a temple built on pure, clean and honest intention can never be dismantled.
- A great master lives inside us all. One must only call upon his or her wisdom and listen closely.
- If you are not thinking great thoughts you are not doing great things.
- Rock the very core of your existence. Take chances and shed fear. Take monumental leaps of faith, rise up, and live your life out loud.
- Never discard any event in your life as un-purposeful. There is a reason for everything.

May 14, 2012 - Original Backpackers Hostel, Sydney, Australia

Upon check-in I was greeted with stark news: The credit card used for my reservation was declined. The somber report felt like I was dropped into a black hole without warning. I might as well have been a fresh-out-of-boot-camp-soldier heading to the coasts of Normandy on June 6, 1944 (D-day) – I was that nervous. Mortified at the thought of being 8400 miles away from home, alone, having only a mere 80 American dollars in cash to my name, and with no place to stay on a chilly Australian winter's night, I frantically took out my wallet with jittering hands, and jolted out all of my credit cards onto the desk. One by one, all three of my hopes were swiped, and deemed useless. In complete denial I desperately said to myself: "This is impossible I have plenty of funds available on every single card."

Having noticed the look of terror on my ghostly face, Mandy, the bespectacled owner, restored my faith in humanity by offering me a warm bed to sleep on (for the night) without any form of payment. She temporarily put my mind at ease by taking my passport, making a photocopy of it, and handing me a room key with an angelic smile on her face. After tossing my backpack in a cramped area comprised of four bunk beds, I set out on a wild goose chase for an ATM. Countless non refundable hours later in a heightened sense of survival mode, exhausted, and still with no luck of finding an ATM that would relinquish funds, I returned defeated to my shared space and tried to figure out what to do next.

The ominous faux wood digital clock framing faded red numbers in the room reads 5:46 PM, so that meant it was 3:46 AM in Miami. There was no one I could ring at this hour and even worse I had no cell phone service. Realizing the walls to my stomach were sticking to each other because I hadn't eaten since I was on the plane from Fiji countless hours ago, and that I would need to buy a calling card to reach home, I headed back out into the increasingly colder streets to convert the sheer $80 USD I had in my pocket into the much stronger Australian Dollar. Finding a currency exchange shop proved to be a much simpler task than encountering a compassionate ATM .

Flush faced and winded, I gasped a tiny sigh of relief after converting my money. I separated my collapsing stomach walls by burning some cash at a sketchy pizza place, and later I bought a calling card from a Korean lady whose "store" gawks more trinkets than all of the shops in NYC's Chinatown combined. The same instance the clock struck 9 AM back home, I rang my bank. Wasting minutes-upon-minutes of precious time proved easy when I was actively dodging the automated voice that "really" wants to help but is entirely useless in a dire situation like this. In what felt like going through a mind -boggling labyrinth designed to test the IQ of a super genius while doing the hula hoop, I, *At Last* (cue Etta James) connected with a live person on the line. After spending nearly 1000 seconds explaining my urgency to the uninterested sleepy female on the phone, she scanned my accounts, and confirmed that my funds are indeed available and that all my cards have been cleared for use in Australia. Overjoyed with the good news, I slammed the chunky ol' payphone without saying a proper goodbye to little Ms. Sleepyhead and meteorically dashed toward the nearest ATM (again). I eagerly stuffed my cards into every bank machine in the whole of the Kings Cross area but once more they showed no mercy.

I was completely demoralized by the situation, and I called my lifeline, my little sister, Karina. I embarrassingly asked her to wire me $400 USD. Within minutes the life-saving funds arrived at the Western Union just outside the Kings Kross metro station and I breathed a huge sigh of absolute relief. With a little cash to burn, I no longer felt entirely helpless and began the exploration of Sydney. However there was a deeper meaning to all that had just occurred:

Having replayed the tape of every single frightening emotion in my mind, reliving every rattled nerve, I channeled my lesson instantaneously: This experience was all about humility, and vulnerability. It was about allowing myself to be open to the aide of others by having to be humble; something I had never felt the need to do before because I was always so "self-sufficient". Interminably egotistical, I disguised it by taking great "pride" in being able to sustain my necessities. I never asked for anyone's help even during times when I desperately needed it, and for once in my life I had to surrender. My EGO had no choice but to deflate itself through vulnerability (the teachings of Renee Brown instantly come to mind). Certainly not accepting the aide from others crutched my spiritual growth to date. For as much as I want to be a constant provider, and help the world, I must also let the world assist me, and in order to receive its help I must remain meek. I have to remain vulnerable. It's universal law.

Spiritual cynicism is a blatant act of ignorance.

May 15, 2012

Sydney's immaculately swept and newly paved streets, impeccably polished high rises that perfectly echo the warm light of the sun, and flawlessly pruned Royal Botanical Gardens with thriving flora and exotic array of wildlife, that would make any flourishing natural wonder of the world green with envy, make it easy to depict it in one word. With model citizens who know how to queue up in a single file line, even if the row of people at the litter free bus stop is 50 deep, leaves me with no other choice than to label it: Utopia. Having morphed itself from a plague infested penal colony of the British Empire to a blooming never-never land, Sydney represents my past, present and desired future.

MAY 16, 2012

The thoughts of today become the realities of tomorrow. Be vigilant of all that crosses your mind.

Those with the least merit are ones with the most excuses.

Simplicity brings about happiness.

SYDNEY OPERA HOUSE – SYDNEY, AUSTRALIA

With arms wide open I embrace the splendor of Sydney's crown jewel. As a child I spent countless hours flipping through pictures of the city in my Encyclopedia Britanica. I remember wishing with all my might that I could visit such an awe-inspiring place one day. Twenty-five years or so later, here I am. It's true: dream, believe, become!

May 18, 2012

Four suns have come and gone, and still my credit cards are not working. I'm convinced Australia has the most heartless ATMs on the planet and doubtless this ominous situation is a divine sign that Sydney, albeit transfixing and all, is not where I am supposed to be. Everything is so freaking expensive for my backpackers' budget. I mean four stinking dollars for tinted soda water, poorly mixed with cheap sugar, sealed in a red aluminum can is just ridiculous. I'm nose-diving the funds my sister has wired me. I need to get the hell out of here, and quickly. I must follow the signs.

CHAPTER 3

A Jack-in-the-Box

A few days of playing financial kamikaze in Australia, and I realized that the profound spiritual knowledge I was seeking was not going to be found in the utopia down under. I knew that I needed to be in the most austere of places. I had to be amongst poverty-stricken people and be shaken to my core. My soul wanted nothing more than to be in the mystical lands of Buddhism. Yearning to walk on streets where throngs of monks are rampant, I bought my fourth one-way ticket, from Sydney, Australia to Kuala Lumpor, Malaysia. I had no clue that the biggest lessons of my life were about to be unveiled.

MAY 19, 2012 - KUALA LUMPOR

Unbeknownst to me, I showed up to Kuala Lumpor on one of the city's biggest festival nights! The revelry is called the "Colours of Malaysia" and rightfully so. It is orchestrated by the Malaysian Tourism Board to showcase the cultural rainbow the country has to offer. The bustling downtown streets are brought to a halt, allowing exuberantly decorated floats to sway before the stargazed crowd of thousands, while thunderous marching bands, sizzling food stalls, spirited dancers, towering stilt walkers, and hooting motorcycles flood every empty crevice. The energy in the air is absolutely electrifying! Malaysia strikes it big in my heart.

MAY 20, 2012 MASJID JAMEK – KUALA LUMPOR, MALAYSIA

With my arms and mind wide open I visited a mosque and was educated on the religion of Islam by a local student, Mohd Naim Bin Abudullah. Before entering, I was asked to put on a Kaftan in order to cover up my bare arms and legs. Twenty-three-year-old Mohd told me that the word "Masjid" means mosque. He instructed me on the cleansing rituals that must be done before prayer. One must wash their face, hands and feet in order to remove negativity. After taking a few shoeless laps around the mosque with eager Mohd by my side (shoes are not allowed inside — they are seen as carriers of dirt, germs, and negativity) we sat down in a quiet area where he would educate me some more.

He said that on Sundays he and many other practitioners come out to feed the homeless of "KL" (Kuala Lumpor) because Mohamed the prophet teaches them to share and assist others in need. He also explained one of the reasons Muslims fast: It is so that they can understand the hunger and starvation of others. He further related that a Muslim must not overeat, rather they should only consume what they need; and they pray five times a day. I was astounded and overwhelmed by the tremendous wealth of knowledge Mohd continued to share with me, and I offered him some money as a way of thanking him. He politely refused the cash, and his only request was that I spread the good word about the people of Malaysia.

THE EMBASSY OF VIETNAM IN KUALA LUMPOR

When I first started thinking about this journey I was always especially drawn to the bewitching allure of Vietnam. Today, coincidentally, I walked by the Vietnamese embassy, and I decided to show up unannounced, knock on the door and apply for a visa.

MAY 22, 2012

I fell for the classic bait and switch "foot massage" by the Chinese lady on the sketchy side street dubbed "massage row". You'd think I would've gotten the hint by her hookerish makeup and attire (I'm not judging her, it was a fact, and if you keep reading I'll tell you why) and if her hooker looks (tattooed eyebrows, super-short lyrca skirt, tube top with NO BRA) didn't give it away, you'd think I would have picked up on her intentions when I accepted her "foot massage" invite for a 25 MR (Malaysian Ringit, which is equal to about $8) and she lead me up a grimy and dimly lit staircase that opened up to a room filled with emancipated beds that are easily concealed by the shifting of mismatched curtains that are draped from the ceiling (think of it like a hospital). Well, naïve me didn't pick up on any of that. I still thought I was getting a "foot massage". It took about 15 minutes of this bordering 30s woman massaging my feet and telling me in her broken English that she's not good at "fooo massah" and suggesting that she massage my penis instead by pointing at my groin, smiling, and saying "massah" for me to understand exactly the service she performed. Only then did it finally hit me! I'd accidentally landed in a happy ending massage parlor imprecisely advertised as a foot massage place! At that point I declined her offer. She wasn't very happy with me because she needed the money and made a zero sign with her hand (as if she had 0 cash) and frowned intently at me. I quickly got up and gave her an extra 10 MR for her mediocre foot service.

MAY 23, 2012

My hero for today is this blind, elderly Muslim woman who was singing for money on the streets of Kuala Lumpor. She had the volume on her badly bruised, wooden speaker box cranked up high, and chanted like an angel as she shook her tambourine to the melodic strains of Malay music. She instantly brought me to tears. I thought about how fortunate I was and how easy life has been for me compared to the life of this woman and that of the multitude of others in Malaysia. I felt reverent appreciation for all that I had. Without ever knowing who I was this hero etches an eternal mark on the blueprint of my soul.

MAY 24, 2012

One of the hardest moments in one's life is when you realize who you truly are within and what you're destined to do with your existence, but no one else sees or believes it. During these moments you find yourself entirely alone, misunderstood by almost everyone, and no one truly understands you. You blame others for not seeing what you see, not only in yourself, but in themselves as well. You don't get why they don't get you.

If you are currently awakening to this, my advice to you is the following: Don't blame a single person. Don't wait for anyone to validate the boundless soul you are. Tap into your faith for unlimited spiritual power, support and strength. Read about the greatest minds that ever existed. When you do you'll quickly realize that they taught and spoke of spirituality in one way or another. When these brilliant minds were considered "outcasts" by society, they turned to something greater and deeper within themselves to keep them going. The results created by these "outcasts" and "dreamers" prove themselves because they produced timeless paintings, sculptures and musical pieces that will continue to awe and inspire the human race for as long as we exist. These minds also became presidents of nations, saints, they invented electricity, abolished slavery, wrote magnificent books, created such things such as democracy, religions, aqueducts, airplanes, cars, space ships; the list goes on and on and on...

And for those of you into pop culture, who is the first "person" most celebrities thank for their success when they win an award? It's not a coincidence! So whether you want to build a rocket ship and go to Mars, or be an amazing mother, and you're in need of strength and support to keep fighting, turn to the Universe inside of yourself for guidance and power. It will never abandon you, nor will it believe that you can't be all that you can be, because after all it created you. If you keep believing in yourself long enough, stay focused and dedicated to your dream, people will eventually see the supernova that you know you are and that you were born to be.

May 26, 2012 - War Remnants Museum, Ho Chi Minh City (Saigon) Vietnam

This sojourn is forever transforming my existence on this planet. Here is Lee Van O; he is 19 years old. Born without eyes, he is a product of the aftermath left behind by traces of the chemicals known as Agent Orange that were used during the Vietnam War. He plays music on the keyboard so he can share his happiness with the world he will never see. I am once again brought to tears by an absolute stranger, and humbled by his presence. Lee Van O's superhuman resilience bulldozes the walls of limitations in my mind. He unknowingly becomes the second hero of my journey.

I had $90 or so a few minutes ago, then I exchanged them for Vietnamese currency, and I now have 1,900,000 VND (Vietnamese Dong). I'm not sure how far that will get me, but it sounded nice when the cashier said, "Here are one million, nine hundred thousand Dong." This is what being a millionaire must feel like.

May 27, 2012

I was up at daybreak and Saigon was already fiercely buzzing. The relentless murmur from the deluge of mopeds that zip most of her twelve million inhabitants across town dominates the air, and makes one feel like there is a swarm of locusts pervading the city. My goal for today was to leap on one of those minibikes and eyeball as many pagodas as I could. After quickly striking a shady deal smack-in-the-middle of the street with a gypsy moped driver, Tanni, I hopped on his backseat, and asked him to take me to all the pagodas he knew of. I spent the next four hours enveloped in an enchanting spell that grew more whimsical as the day progressed. Like unwrapping big boxed presents on a birthday, one after the other, every pagoda kept striking the chords of my utmost happiness. The flamboyant colors painted on hundreds of statues of all sizes, exotic smells of burning incense, watching barefoot devotes on their hands and knees intensely praying, along with the flickering of candles and neon lights overwhelmed my senses. This dazzling statute of young Buddha was one of the many hidden treasures I found.

MAY 28, 2012

The new colors of old Saigon. I don't care about politics, I'm more interested in people, and the people of Vietnam have by far exceeded my expectations for hospitality and genuine kindness. The young kids flash peace signs at you from their mopeds, while the ones you walk by on the streets stop you to ask about your opinion of their country. The men all want to take you for a ride on their minibikes to earn a few bucks (which I have now accepted twice and it's freaking thrilling to say the least). The women here are the best sales force I have ever seen. They will switch up a deal on you and make you buy a sack of crap in a fraction of a heartbeat, and you will walk away happier than Don

35

Quixote on his first sally. The two most used English words here are "No Problem" because the Vietnamese can solve anything. With this said I proudly wear this flag.

Somehow this journey is ushering me into poorer and even worse, war-stricken nations. Ironically some of these countries house the world's holiest sites, like Cambodia for example. Tomorrow I will pack my bag and take a bus over the border to Phnom Penh, the capital of Cambodia. There I will learn about elementary schools converted into torture centers, rice fields immersed in blood due to the assassination of hundreds of thousands of innocent human beings. From there I will travel to the Temples of Angkor, which are considered to be one of the most impressive ancient and religious sites on earth, matched only by a few other places on this planet such as Machu Picchu in Peru, or Petra in Jordan. I'm still unaware of my entire purpose of this path, but I gladly accept my mission blindly; I have total faith that this and only this, is what I'm supposed to be doing with my existence at this moment.

MAY 29, 2012 – PHNOM PENH, CAMBODIA

We are all prisms of light, and our sole duty is to refract out the light the Universe provides us in the colors of patience, kindness, love, sincerity, hope, loyalty, sharing, and faith. The more light you "refract" the more light will enter your life. There is no limit to the amount of your light one can receive, there is only a limit to the amount of light one wishes to share.

Phnom Penh sucker punches me with delight when I find that its streets are sprinkled with monks draped in deep orange colored robes at every turn. One can only feel safe and at peace in such a place where this is a reality.

MAY 30, 2012. OUTSIDE THE TUOL SLENG GENOCIDE MUSEUM IN PHNOM PENH, CAMBODIA

My hero for today is this 6-year-old girl hawking scarves, bracelets, and pirated DVDs just outside the Genocide Museum on the streets of Phnom Penh. Her English was perfect, and her sales skills were equivalent to that of the adult Vietnamese women which as we know are Grade A sellers. Her little purse is stuffed with the cash she's rightfully earned. She closes the deal by challenging you to a game of paper, rock, scissors. If she wins you pay $1 more for the item. If she loses you pay $1 less. We played and my rock smashed her scissors. And even though I ardently insisted, she refused to take the dollar "tip" I offered her.

MAY 31, 2012

New York City has its famed Yellow Crown Victoria taxis. Berlin is notorious for its fleet of Mercedes Benz cabs. Phnom Penh's answer to all that is: the "Tuk-Tuk", a moped with a chariot attached. As I was whisked away in my own private carriage heading toward the Choeng EK-Killing Fields, I snapped a picture of the view.

MAGIC TREE .. THE TREE WAS USED AS
A TOOL TO HANG A LOUDSPEAKER WHICH
MAKE SOUND LOUDER TO AVOID THE MOAN
OF VICTIMS WHILE THEY WERE BEING EXECUTED

MAY 31, 2012 – CHOEUNG EK - KILLING FIELDS, PHNOM PENH, CAMBODIA.

There is no magic here, only sorrow. Read with prudence as this is a true macabre story that occurred in our lifetime. From about 1975 to 1979 Cambodia lost close to a quarter of its population (somewhere over a million people) to genocide under the dictatorship of Pol Pot.

Pol Pot wanted to create a new society and conducted purges to eliminate the remnants of what he believed to be the old society. Pol Pot's old society consisted of anyone from Buddhist monks to doctors, teachers (the religious and educated were considered unworthy), or anyone else who was thought to be disloyal. The victims were herded to this field outside of the city, lined up in rows and assassinated. When bullets became too expensive they were bludgeoned with axes, or even had their necks sliced open with the rigid edges of a Palm tree branch. To add to the terror of the history of this gut-wrenching place I encountered remnants of the victims' bones, teeth, and deteriorated clothing items embedded in the anguished soil while abhorrently tip-toeing along the fields.

Phnom Penh is heavy on the heart and harsh on the eyes. Although it has wonderful golden palaces and silver roofed pagodas, the city's two main attractions are still "The Killing Fields" and "The Genocide Museum". What happened here is horrific and the fact that it occurred in a not-so-distant past is what leaves a macabre vestige. The energy (at times) feels very heavy, making you just wanna run home or break down into tears.

But when you usher in the warmth of its people, you realize that you are helping rebuild a nation that went through a recent "ethnic cleansing". You accept the guilt you feel inside and just keep going. The weight in your soul is a small cross to bear. The rewards are limitless smiles from its people and assurance that you are making a tiny contribution to something greater than just a good time for yourself, and that feels grander than anything you have ever bought.

JUNE 1, 2012 – SIEM REAP CAMBODIA

Tired, dirty, and dehydrated from a very warm and dusty four-hour bus ride from Phnom Penh to Siem Reap on the worst dirt road I have ever traveled in my entire life, I find myself somewhere in the middle of Cambodia. Not entirely sure as to where I am in the world, I find that I am also still very much unnerved from visiting the Killing Fields yesterday. I've never been this far away from home alone and for this long of time. I have pushed myself extremely far out of my comfort zone.

If I were a steel trap, this would definitely be the point were the coils have been wound so tightly it's about to give…

The realization of one's dreams mean nothing at all without someone special next to you to share the experience with.

With this said, I've come to the conclusion that even though I can reach the Great Wall of China and the Taj Mahal in just a few weeks, I'm strongly considering saving the experiences to share them with that special someone, my family, or just my plain ol' friends.

It took for me to travel through three continents and be in the heart of one of the poorest and most war-stricken nations on earth to learn a very important lesson in life, and it's about having someone around you to share special moments with. It's about being selfless and waiting for the right person and/or persons to share the right moments, even though you can experience them alone. It's about knowing how to at least begin to love someone else other than yourself, even if they are not present.

I now find it too selfish and egotistical to keep going at this alone. I want to save some of these awe-inspiring experiences so that they may gift someone else as well, because I've also learned that our true happiness lies in the happiness of others and NOT JUST IN OUR OWN.

Like a jack-in-the-box springing forward with all its excitement, I found the answer to the question about the importance of partnerships that I didn't know I was asking, bursting right through my soul.

June 2, 2012 – Temples of Angkor Wat, Siem Reap, Cambodia

Jittery anticipation was building in every bone of my body as the never ending "putt-putt" sound from the struggling motor of the Tuk-Tuk I was on, kept my nerves riled. As we distanced ourselves farther from the small, dusty and desolate town of Siem Reap and deeper into the Cambodian wilderness on yet another frightening dirt road, Lucky, the driver, smiled and told me not to worry — he sensed my nervousness. He reassured my frantic looking self by proudly advising me that he'd recently given a full body tune-up to his muddy "made in Vietnam" motorbike, and further told me that he'd driven this rain beaten path for his entire life, and that no one else was as familiar with it as him. He closed his reassurance sales pitch by reminding me of his name, "Lucky". So there was really no need to worry as "luck" was on my side.

The Temples of Angkor are beyond massive and since they're so deeply tucked away in the lush, hot, and humid Cambodian jungle one has no idea as to the magnitude of this monolithic and divine site until one reaches its main entrance. After driving out of the forest and into the open space that encircles Angkor, I got my first glimpse of the world's largest religious monument. Immediately I sensed a profound shift from within. I couldn't quite put my finger on it just then but I knew something was stirred in my soul at the very site of this archaeological and spiritual marvel. It felt like a gut wrenching déjà vu. The psychic in Miami was correct; I am visiting the lands of past lives. This feeling of surety confirms this: "I" have been to these sacred grounds before.

I anxiously hopped off the Tuk-Tuk and stepped on the stone bridge that hovers over the massive moat surrounding the temples, and was overcome with visions of my past. The farther I walked along this gateway of revelations the clearer the picture of my life mistakes became. I saw the faces of the people whom I'd hurt during my drinking and drug abuse days parading in front of my eyes. The deeper I penetrated the labyrinth of temples of which tally up to a combined total of 1000, the more profound the weight of yesteryear became on my soul. As if lead were flowing through my body the energy only continued to get heavier and heavier as I helplessly wove through some of the stone shrines that served as the scenic backdrop for *Lara Croft Tomb Raider;* desperately trying to find an escape. The merciless jungle sun and the boggy marshland air was also unbearable — I finally surrendered to the moment.

I sobbed as if a close relative had passed, repenting for all my misdoings. All the lies I told to excuse my addictions, all the unnecessary fights I'd caused in my relationships just to go out, have a drink, and a bump, were sitting right in my face. Once again I knew I needed to act fast. I reached for my iPhone from a sagging pocket and typed in all the names of the faces who had just appeared to me. I made a vow to reach out to them. I promised I would contact every single person no matter how distant in the past they were and ask for their forgiveness. My vagabond soul was on its knees, intensely rattling a metal can, supplicating closure at a deafening level.

Shortly after punching the names into a humid glass screen, I found an exit, and lo-and-behold my "lucky Tuk-Tuk" driver was there waiting for me with his warm, broken tooth smile, and motor bike *putt-putting* away. When I arrived at the seven dollar a night guesthouse where I was staying, the first thing I did was fuss with a cracked power button on the rickety wall AC. After a few MacGuyver moves I got the AC running, then fired off my apology emails. They were precise, I didn't sugarcoat my mistakes. "I'm sorry for being so selfish", said the first line of one, and within minutes I was done. Hours later everyone had surprisingly responded and granted me their forgiveness. I felt a sense of closure; my panhandling soul had thrown away its tin cup, muffled its cries, and found itself proudly back on its feet. I was ready to continue on my journey.

But before forging ahead I sat back and reflected on the invaluable life lessons this cathartic happenstance brought upon me: Redemption, we are all capable of it, and we must find those who we've hurt, and ask them for their forgiveness. Without recognizing our mistakes and not redeeming ourselves we cannot further progress down the spiritual path. On the other side of the same token: Forgiveness, we must pardon those who have hurt us to clear our conscious of all resentment. Rancor will infest our souls if we cling to it, mercilessly decomposing at any spiritual advancement we think we've made.

CHAPTER 4

The Old World Brings New Lessons

My first reaction upon arrival was to chuckle. It's kind of like what a mischievous and sugar addicted boy would do after getting away with eating that cookie his parents told him to not even dare put his hands on. I asked myself, "What the heck am I doing in Abu Dhabi?" In what felt like a blink of an eye so far, I have managed to use eight different currencies, cross the Pacific Ocean, set foot on Australia, backpack a section of Southeast Asia, fly over the entire belly of India and land in the Middle East. And with a connecting flight to Germany in a few hours, and a third connecting flight to Ibiza, Spain in about fifteen hours, I see the bigger picture.

The metaphor that I am about to use feels like it was handed to me on a silver platter. It was Divinely catered. I told myself, "Look how far you have traveled, and not just physically. Analyze the distance you have voyaged spiritually." Having been a tormented soul haunted by suicidal thoughts a few months back to now being in perfect harmony with my existence, the physical miles traveled were clearly The Divine's way of showing me the spiritual miles I'd conquered. I have grown significantly in such a short time.

This thought openly invites the chills to feverishly run up and down my spine. The back and forth motion is reminiscent of a sold-out crowd in a football stadium doing the wave over and over again, just after a seemingly impossible touchdown. The sensations are brought to a screeching halt by the sound of a heavily accented female voice coming through a loud crackling speaker that says: "Now boarding Etihad Airways flight number 23 to Dusseldorf, Germany." That's my plane!

June 10, 2012 - Ibiza, Spain

The White Isle, queen of the Balearics, I had yearned for this encounter for as long as I could remember. The countless stories I've heard of the healing presence one feels the very second the double glass doors of the tiny airport pry open, fall short. I wasn't prepared to be captivated with such serenity. As if I was Ponce de Leon uncovering the Fountain of Youth, after his lifelong quest to find it, I rejoiced at the discovery of the rejuvenating energy that can only be felt on the magic island.

Home to an uncanny islet called "Es Vedra" which esoteric myths claim hosts one of the planet's highest magnetic points, and considered a spiritual hotbed by mystics who believe it has healing powers, it's without wonder I was drawn here. After having gouged out lifetimes of bad karma during my exploration of The Temples of Angkor Wat, this was exactly where I needed to be in order to mend the gushing holes that remained in my soul.

June 11, 2012

Find your inner Aurora Borealis. Seek out your soul's superior version of the Northern Lights and let them shine through your skin. You'll see that people around you will notice the dance of the invisible light display emanating from within you. You'll find that they respond just as they do when they see a natural phenomenon of extreme beauty. They'll be in total awe of your presence and you'll inspire them to seek their very own inner magic.

June 12, 2012

Let us become peddlers of the propaganda of love. Let us unite and become modern day abolitionists working to free the world from the slavery of hate. Let us build multiple legions of love armed with missionaries of dance, laughter, freedom, art and music all fighting for the same cause, which is to end the negativity. Let us incite massive love riots sparked by the flame of a miracle. Let us become ambassadors of infinite goodwill. Let us dream, for a dream is what will save us all.

June 13, 2012

You can only dress truth in lies for so long. At some point the fiery crowd of fact will come toward you and rip the beautifully tailored suit of deceit you have so selfishly made to hide everything you are afraid of showing, right off your body. Time, karma and truth are all allies, working against this cheap costume of falsehood; they will leave you naked in your reality. Why not slowly begin to peel it off right now, and start tailoring one made of an organic nonperishable item called the truth.

June 15, 2012

I hold a very beloved place in my heart for Vienna. For she was the city where I first experienced the miraculous sensations of awe and wonder that a spiritual awakening brings. The imperial city has been coming to mind a lot lately. She has been sending me telepathic messages beckoning my return. In response to her cosmic-like communication attempts I've spent most of the day online, trying to find my way back to her loving embrace for the next month, maybe longer.

June 16, 2012

I must admit I'm one hell of a wildcard these days. I'm probably deemed a reckless traveler by most, but I've no interest in what others' thoughts of me are (if so I would've never turned over my business, broken my lease, sold most of my worldly possessions that included my matador red Lexus, to go on this journey). Honestly I've never felt truer to my soul nor have I ever felt more alive in my life before (by alive I mean afraid, happy, rattled, anxious, peaceful, joyous, sad and more).

I attest that being a global pilgrim jumping from continent to continent in search of something that's only tangible by the soul puts you on an emotional roller coaster of epic proportions. Just as the physical miles traveled are monumental so is the range of sentiments one goes through. I have witnessed myself at my very best, testified to my absolute worst, and juried it all. From this I have grown tremendously.

I am having the experience of a lifetime that many dream of, but few attain. For this to happen it required taking great risks, complete disavowal of all my fears, and incalculable amounts of faith in The Divine. When my dying day arrives and my life flashes before my eyes I will have no regrets in what I have done.

June 17, 2012

I have exorcised all of the demons from my past. The monsters that lurked in the shadows of my soul, who were hell-bent on dragging me down with them, have dissipated. Light has been cast. I am perfectly comfortable being the voice of sobriety. Through abysmal introspection I have learned from all of my mistakes and I've made the apologies to those who deserved one from me. There are zero messes left for me to clean up. Like a painter with a blank canvas, I am the proud owner of a clean slate to start living anew. I'm eager to paint a beautiful new existence. I'm 150% ready to catapult my being forward, and I'm more than willing to embrace everything that comes my way. It is clearer than the Red Sea that this journey has not ended; instead it is only going in the direction it was destined. Like a Phoenix soaring above the ashes, I have risen.

June 18, 2012 – Barcelona, Spain

Barcelona is one of those places you instantly want to pen home about. It has the power to incite romance in the most callous of hearts. I don't think anyone can come here and not help but want to get lost in its streets, and roam them aimlessly under the spell they cast upon you. This beguiling metropolis ideally set on the Balearic Sea, ping-pongs my emotions to-and-fro in jubilance and exhilaration. As if I were its most valuable prisoner of war, BCN (as some refer to the city) captivates my excitement, and for not even a half second does it ever attempt to set it free.

June 20, 2012 – Museu Picasso

Encountering the war chest of Pablo Picasso's art work, face to canvas, instantly subjects you to falling under the puppetry of his grandiose influence. With over 3500 pieces by Picasso in this museum alone, I was forced to ask myself, "How's it possible that one man could create so much?" Instantly, it dawns upon me: He dedicated every waking moment to his passion. And in doing so, he left behind a legacy of beauty that will inspire humanity for all time. Honestly I couldn't think of a better way to part from this big blue marble we call Earth, than by leaving it with the creations of our passions. Whether it'd be through artwork, writing, dedication to the sciences, nursing the sick, educating the young, or raising children, we can all strive to be Picassos.

When I realized that happiness is not based on an exterior condition and I discovered that I was always in complete control of it, I no longer found the need to blame someone or something else when I was unhappy. I now understand that in the state of just being lie all the answers to my happiness, so I never stray too far from it. To be is to be happy.

June 21, 2012

I'm in seventh heaven with just being. I desire nothing but to just be. I have never reached this sense of beatitude before. If I had the ability to buy anything in the world right now I wouldn't because I have no desire for anything that can be purchased. I posses all I require. My only desire is to wake up and live.

June 23, 2012 – La Rambla

Less than 24 hours left in Barcelona and once again that bittersweet sensation of an imminent departure is overtaking me. I have become all too accustomed to this feeling of loving and letting go, loving and leaving before things plateau. However the perpetual soul searcher in me found a lesson to be learned from it. The lesson is about impermanence and learning to accept that everything in life has a cycle with a beginning and heartbreakingly an end. Nothing, absolutely nothing, is forever. Even Rome crumbled.

Acceptance of impermanence teaches that when you have something in your life that is worthwhile you must enjoy it, respect it, cherish it, treasure it and hold on to it for as long as you can. Treat it as if you were going to lose it because someday you will. It sounds pretty grim but if you accept this as a fact you will value everything in your life a lot more, and you will also hurt a whole lot less once it's gone. IMPERMANENCE is the only thing that is permanent.

June 24, 2012

I am a diehard graffiti enthusiast. To me, graffiti speaks the unfiltered truth. Here it reads "Casa sin gente, gente sin casa" which translates into "homes without people, people without out homes". This is a clear tell-all of the housing crisis that has been rocking the privileged world since 2008. This picture further proves a long-running theory of mine, that if you really want to know what is going on in the world around you get off the Internet, trash your newspapers and go read the walls of your city. There you will find the uncensored truth written by the most daring of souls who risk jail time and fines in order to tell you just how they feel about something.

June 25, 2012 - Pyrenees Mountains, France

Teaching a faithless person to believe in The Divine is a difficult task. It's like leading a blind person to the mountains. You know that they are there but they can't see them. Your only hope is that they stand in silence long enough so that they may feel the presence of the giants that they are surrounded by.

June 25, 2012 - Milan, Italy

Slowly rolling into Milan after a 16-hour train ride from Barcelona, my first impression of the city came from its glass skyscrapers, graffiti-riddled ghettos, and silhouettes of cathedrals fiercely competing with the smoke puffing pipes of its factories. This was not exactly what I have in mind when I envision a European city. But Milan is its own animal, and embodies all of Italy's struggles, and triumphs; for this alone it should be heavily applauded and deeply admired. Through its sky piercing buildings and crumbling facades this city offers a window to my soul. Not entirely sure of its future, it demonstrates faith in itself by building for it. All the while it tries to console a deteriorating past.

In experiencing having utterly nothing you tend to find absolutely everything. The beauty of understanding that simplicity is sheer happiness is very well undermined by most people who are inanely clueless about the treasures that lie within themselves. They seek happiness outside of themselves because they know not any better. They compromise their values and true selves by chasing after fading stars, only to find that once they have seemingly grabbed these stars they are nothing but dust. Then again, who has taught them differently?

June 26, 2012

Your most prized treasures are the ones that cannot be photographed or stolen because they are stored deeply inside of you. The Crown Jewels-of-Crown-Jewels are found in the Tower of the Soul.

CANAL DISTRICT, MILAN

Burst the levees that hold back universal flow into your soul. Erect canals that channel the divine energy and sublime goodness of the Universe directly into your heart.

The mind will never fully understand that which the soul desires. This is why it's crucial to listen to and follow your heart at all costs.

To live a resplendent existence one must have a grandiose faith. One must have a supreme belief in self and a far superior conviction that the here and now is Divinely catered.

The valiant characters who have crossed my path along the way have been the most vital part of this transformative experience. They are all living, breathing stories of inspiration. Here you have a sole protestor in his mid to late 60s standing in front of an Italian governmental building. He's speaking out against what he feels is a communist agenda in the Italian government. Whether he is "right" and even if he is "wrong" it is of no importance to me. What I find inspiring is the fire that gets him out of bed to hang a sign around his neck, and solemnly stand in front of a building for hours-upon-hours in the unforgiving Milan summer heat. He becomes the fourth hero in my journey.

June 27, 2012

Today I asked myself, "Has it been 3 days since I got here?" Then I counted with my fingers and realized that yes it has been 3 days: Monday 1, Tuesday 2, Wednesday 3. If you have been to Milan you can say that 3 days is enough to get the gist of this city. Especially if you are like me and spend about 12 to 15 hour days sightseeing and exploring. This leaves me with four days to get to my beloved summer home of Vienna.

After a few hours of searching for the best route to Vienna from Milan I found that flying via Istanbul is the cheapest way. It turns out the most cost-efficient route to get to Vienna and to kill four days at the same time is to fly to Turkey. So in 12 hours I'm strapping on my backpack one more time, trading in the cathedrals for mosques and heading to Istanbul till Sunday night.

I may have negated my eyes to the Taj Mahal and the Great Wall of China for now, but I find it completely illogical to deny myself the experience of Hagia Sophia and everything else that is Istanbul.

June 28, 2012 – Istanbul, Turkey

I'm expecting to see Aladdin zipping between the countless minarets of the mosque adorned sky, riding on his magic carpet, at any second now. I am certain that if I scour the multitude of shops in the colorful and seemingly endless labyrinth locals call the Grand Bazaar, I will find someone willing to sell me a genie in a bottle. Women covered in black burqas, holy chants emanating from speakers purposely placed outside the abounding mosques, tightly wedged buildings on cobblestone streets so jam-packed that I can't fit a dime in the space between the next person and myself, serve as part of the full-on assault Istanbul has waged on my senses.

As I try and take this all in, a man wearing a red, cup-shaped hat, peddling five glasses of steaming hot Turkish tea on silver platter, pushes me to the side. Breathing in the scents of summer air, wilderness, and freedom, I realize that the smells are of the spices that were catalysts for war, and built empires during the spice trade. I turn around and my eyes crash into a sea of rainbows; there are condiments for sale in every color imaginable. I don't ever want this moment to end.

I find it extremely peculiar that many have no issues in glorifying products as the source of their happiness, yet when it comes to speaking about finding the joy within and walking the spiritual path many silence themselves out of fear of what others may think of them, or unfairly judge those who do speak of the light. This is completely unnatural. It's absurd and lunatic. It's a clear sign of a societal mental disorder that is leading to the pillaging of our last worldly resources and unless we turn this thought process around, it will eventually wipe us all out. This spiritual pollution needs to be cleaned up and it can only be done if we all start waking from this absurd notion that glamour and material are the only source of our happiness. Don't get me wrong, it's good to have good things, but don't let those good things make you think that the fact of having them makes you "good".

June 29, 2012

You know those very rare nights in your life when you unintentionally break dawn because you are having the time of your life, and you completely lost track of time? Tonight was one of them. Here's to unexpected, unsolicited magic and newfound friends in foreign lands.

The choices in life can be seen as a series of liquids contained inside jars. Envision these jars spread out on a multi-level shelf. Now imagine that these liquid filled jugs are clearly marked with poison, addiction, mediocrity, laziness, depression, and boredom, to name a few. The containers labeled with the most hazardous ingredients will always be found on the lower level of this shelf of life. Easy to reach, most people spend a lifetime grabbing and drinking from these elixirs. Most will die not knowing what the other liquids on the upper shelves taste like simply because they failed to want to reach a little higher. They will die not knowing what triumph, virtue, happiness, joy, peace, and serenity taste like.

59

Don't be one of these people. Reach for the highest jar on the shelf and if you can't grab it on your own there's a container conveniently placed in the middle that everyone can reach labeled "faith". Drink from that one first and see how meteorically you're able to reach all the other items that are way up high.

Be the paste that people copy, not a copy paste. Live an authentic life dictated by you and only you. Remember it has always been the original thinkers and doers who have changed the world. It has always been that one person brave enough to choose differently who forever changed the course of humanity.

June 30, 2012 – Blue Mosque

The imagination of an architect is something I've curiously always wanted to peer into. How do they dream up their creations? What inspires them to produce such masterful works of art? As I am drowned in an ocean of perfectly situated shiny white and blue tiles encircling over 200 intricately designed stained glass windows, and dwarfed beyond imagination by the sheer magnitude of the breathtaking columns from the belly of one of the pride and joys of the Turks, I am lead to these thoughts: Our imaginations are boundless. They have the power to liberate us from all our troubles. They present a myriad of opportunities to create something divine, and without them we would still be living like Neanderthals. Everything that is now a reality was birthed in imagination, this is fact.

I choose to wander in imagination on a daily basis because in it I have found a prolific world of marvel and an infinite ocean of creativity. Imagination is the womb of our reality.

June 30, 2012 - Hagia Sofia, Istanbul, Turkey

It was prophesized that this journey's purpose would be that of following the footsteps of past lives. Even though I received a forewarning of this many months ago by the clairvoyant in Miami, I still manage to stun myself with how I've been able to navigate the streets of cities in foreign lands that I have never been to, without speaking the language, using a map, or even having a guide book handy. Like a magnet in a junkyard, I have connected with all that has crossed my path. This couldn't be truer in Istanbul where I was drawn to the Hagia Sofia instantaneously. In just one hour of being in Turkey I managed to find my hotel, check in, leave my bag, and gravitate to this marvel without ever taking a cab, asking for directions, or pausing to think.

CHAPTER 5

A Pilgrims Puzzle

I feel like a huge branch from the wisdom tree has abruptly fallen, cracking open my skull, and feeding it with Divine intelligence. Life has become ever so clear. I sense that I've gotten to the point on this pilgrimage, across Planet Earth, where I am about to reach my metaphorical Mecca. I am certain that just over today's horizon or on the next sunset I will flood the levees of blockage with so much intent, giving them no choice but to helplessly burst open and show me the final answers to the life questions ("Who am I? What do I do with my existence?"), that I have been so desperately seeking. Vienna, the imperial city where my spiritual renaissance was birthed, will be the grand stage where these answers act out their reveal.

Dear Vienna,

There is something about us that reverberates at deafening volumes in the abyss of my being. It is an understood, unspoken tongue amongst the energy I sustain inside me, and the light that runs way down through your "mint" avenues. I have a sense of being inside of you but I've yet to come. This impenetrable sensation of belonging leaves me with a flaming question about our connection, and as to why I was guided toward your life-giving embrace once more. Having all but thrown my shirt on the table, here I'm telling you that we've only thirty, possibly sixty days, to figure this affaire de coeur out. I plead your disclosure of anything and everything I must assimilate from you in the most resplendent and benevolent fashion that only you my beloved Vienna can deliver.

Please bring me the truths I am intently seeking loudly and clearly. Embed them in the melodies of your philharmonic, as I lend a sharp ear from the cheap seats in the back. Spray-paint them on the graffiti riddled walls of the blue river that inspired Johann Strauss to compose one of the greatest waltzes of all times, making them visible, as I, without any aim whatsoever, foolishly gaze along its banks. Dispatch signals using the mist inside one of the scores of opulent smoke filled cafes as once again, I, without a hope, sit there in struggle, shamefully penning out exactly why it is I feel so passionate about us. Disguise them in the rattling of your chandeliers while I dance the moon away to the thumping sounds of house music spun inside one of the legions of your palatial estates.

Again we have the limitations of time here. Smash every window of my senses with your enchantment so that when the moment of utter heartbreak comes for us to once again tragically part, I can walk away understanding why it is you who plays such a symbolic role in my existence. Reveal to me that who I am.

July 2, 2012 – Vienna, Austria

To the City of Music,

I was nervous at the thought that the second time around the magic between us would be all but a faint memory; a distant echo in the Grand Canyon of our souls. But you, my dearest queen of the Danube, proved me entirely wrong. Your sorcery is as potent as ever. I've once again surrendered and I'm spellbound by all that is you. Our romance is once again incredibly alive.

My biggest fear in life is not death as that is unavoidable. What I do find chilling and can avoid is not living life richly enough because I'm living it in the shadows of others' opinions.

July 3, 2012

After two months of existing as a global gypsy, I've settled in my new "apartment" which is actually a rundown student dorm. I had no idea that it would be in a crummy dormitory, but then again I didn't care about the details when I booked it with a price tag of $450 per month. As long as it's cheap and in Vienna, I was OK with it, and it's really not so bad.

Julia, the girl with a skin color reminiscent of a Cumulus cloud, whom I unknowingly illegally sublet the place from, made sure every inch of its 45 square feet was spotless before she handed me the keys and jetted off with her boyfriend to China. The petite redhead also made sure that I had the combination to her bike lock so I could freely use her joie de vivre on wheels. The bicycle was the bells and whistles to this place anyway. I'd always envisioned myself drowning out the light of a summer's day by endlessly peddling around a European city on a cruiser bike with a giant metal basket in the front. And as an added bonus, firecracker Julia redounds her nascent career as a shady landlord by leasing me her laptop and speakers for "just" an extra ten Euros per month. Having an apartment in Vienna, a bicycle, and a computer with speakers, I really couldn't be any merrier.

July 4, 2012

"Viva la vie Boheme"

"Bohemianism is the practice of an unconventional lifestyle, often in the company of like-minded people with few permanent ties, involving musical, artistic or literary pursuits. In this context, Bohemians can be wanderers, adventurers or vagabonds." - Wikipedia

86,400 minutes into this herculean adventure, while farming the fruitful crop of a long and fluffy beard on my face, I can say that I've become the embodiment of all that is "Bohemia". Erasing the sun from the sky as I partake in a cafe culture that is UNESCO noteworthy, ruminating and penning those things I voraciously desire, to witnessing the passing of many-a-moons ogling ballets, operas, or strolling the belly of one of the world's most comprehensive cultural centers, this is the life I've always dreamt of. Freedom of this grandeur must be experienced by all human beings.

Long live all that is Bohemian; Vienna forever.

July 5, 2012

This morning I purposely left my umbrella at home so I could walk in the rain. I didn't really rush to my destination either. I absolutely loved feeling every drop hit my skin because they felt like sweet kisses falling from the sky. I was certain that the raindrops were little pecks of love sent from the heavens above in order to tell me everything is just going swell... One after the other, drop after drop, the sky reinforced its love by gifting me with tiny dabs of the world's most precious resource for absolutely nothing in return.

July 6, 2012

The only thing that supersedes the law of impermanence is the love of The Divine. The love of Spirit never changes or goes away. It is always there ceaselessly hovering around us waiting for our acknowledgement. One only need to call upon it to receive its help.

July 7, 2012

I've had plenty of time to think and write about anything and everything these days. However the undertone of this entire journey has been that of the importance of partnerships. I guess for a single 35-year-old man who has always believed in and wanted to stay in love (so far, unsuccessfully) this makes total sense as to why this has become one of the predominant themes along this adventure.

With my spare time, I've wanted to pick apart my past to see all of my mistakes in order to learn about what I did wrong as opposed to looking at what the other person did incorrectly. I've pointed the blame finger toward myself. I also have analyzed and studied those relationships that seem to last and I found the following:

The point of having and being a partner is to be exactly that "a partner" through thick and thin, through the magic and the bullshit. After all you can't have a rainbow without the rain. See where I'm getting at? A partner's duty is to be loyal and faithful. I know that this is a tough one for the guys, but if you want the real lasting deal then you've got to stop thinking the grass is always greener, because it is not. I tell you this from firsthand experience. You also have to commit to communicating with each other honestly and respectfully. Be as open as possible, transparency saves the day every single time. You must value yourself as much as you value your partner. Partnerships take time and effort to create. They are not built overnight, and just because you have a bad moment that doesn't mean you call it off – that just signifies you need to think and see how things can be improved. Relationships require sacrifice, and at times they'll ask us to put the other person's needs in front of our very own. You must also be willing to see past the other's imperfections and love them anyway (I just learned this one recently).

I clearly had not practiced my preachings in the past and this is why I sit here, traveling the world in loneliness, pondering the very essence of all my mishaps in love.

I can tell you that once the sun dies on the final day of this cosmic quest, and I march toward that place called "home", I will be more than ready to construct an everlasting relationship. I will be more than willing to fiercely fight for it and make whatever sacrifices are needed, because after all no matter how people glorify the single life, in the very end we all desire love. The problem is that just that a few of us are actually willing to make the effort it takes to build it, nurture it and keep it forever.

July 8, 2012

When the last party balloon drops, lands on an icky floor, and the light of day becomes blinding, who is there standing beside you? Who are you and what will become of you when the smoke and mirrors are replaced with your reality? When that moment of passion fizzles as they all do, who can you really count on? As your beauty withers into time, realizing that your march toward the inevitable has long begun and you can't reverse the clock, who will march with you? Who will hold your hand? Who will fill the vacuity in your life?

July 9, 2012

Dear Muses,

As much as I love the carnivalesque-type atmosphere of ideas you have going on in my head I can only act upon one at a time. So if you guys could pick a leader and prioritize these wonderful thoughts, then deliver them accordingly, I would greatly appreciate it.

Sincerely,
The management

There are moments in life that are best defined by a song. Today as I watch the sun dip behind the green rolling hills of this imperial city and I look forward to an evening filled with music and art, this song sets the mood for everything that I am feeling inside. It is not necessarily the lyrics but more so the feeling the music and the tone of his voice evoke within me. LONG LIVE BOHEMIA – Café Negro's *In Your Eyes* plays.

The choir of the heart sings much louder than that of the one, in the mind.

July 10, 2012

I'm amused at how I get slightly annoyed at Austrians for not speaking English when I'm in a German speaking country. My belly is full of chuckles seconds after I get a tad bit flurried when they do not understand my Miami/Cuban/American German gibberish. Have you ever heard what "excuse me" sounds like in German? It comes out something like this: EN-CHOO-REE-GUM. So I say, "I'm sorry con EN-CHOO-REE-GUM, but do you speak English?" Their faces immediately go from a blank no thrills central European stare to the most puzzled of looks. I assume they think that I am mad.

It has dawned upon me, let the church bells ring, I've done it! More so I'm still doing it! I'm living a dream by traveling around the world all in one nonstop majestic voyage. It feels like a genie has granted my every wish. Hopping from one continent to another, I've accomplished what only a few months ago seemed like an overwhelming task. I have reaffirmed my belief that there is no such thing as impossible when you're entirely driven and focused on your goals. Anything you want you can have (you can be your own genie), however you can't for a split-second doubt your magic powers and what you are capable of. Never be afraid of taking risks and when life pushes you down you stand right back up with more confidence. Don't ever pay attention to a single word that comes from a negative person because they are only trying to impose their lack of belief in themselves and in the power of the Divine onto you. If you're forced to listen, air seal your lips, floss your ears with what they say, and when they're done toss the string of word crap into forgetfulness. Dream, believe and you will become.

JULY 11, 2012 – BRATISLAVA, SLOVAKIA

The train ride from Vienna to Bratislava is fifty minutes long. These cities are on the top tier of the list that names the world's closest capitals. The distance between them is a mere 40 miles. A round-trip train through the Viennese hinterland and into Slovakian charm is priced at fourteen euros. Taking advantage of their togetherness and budget friendly connection, I eagerly venture into the tiny neighboring country to the east.

Old town Bratislava is a real-life time machine. Immediately teleporting one into a medieval era with its cramped cobblestone walkways, lightly dotted with friars dressed in brown robes that are loosely banded by a knotted rope at the waist. Church bells joyously sing at the hour, on the hour, every hour. Quaint cafes quietly mumble with the voices of a sparingly amount of tourists making a quick pit stop between Vienna and Budapest. The Danube, softly caresses the Slovak capital's river walk offering a place to stroll in absolute serenity.

My perception of what is "far" has been changed drastically. I found myself thinking that distance is nothing when you're willing to travel the miles and enjoy the ride while doing so. No matter how far your dreams may seem, make sure you take steps toward them every day and enjoy the walk. In good time you will get there.

JULY 12, 2012

If those of us who are equipped with flashlights in this cave we call life actually turned them on, it wouldn't be so dark for those who can't afford a flashlight of their own.

Superiority that identifies itself with a material item is a deeply deluded, sick and egotistical thought. Renounce it at all costs. We are not what we own. We are so much more. Shred the veil of deception. The true treasures of life are free and everyone owns them.

July 13, 2012 – Vienna, Austria

Vienna is proving to be a true bastion of culture. My head is spinning incessantly with the immutable barrage of cultural manifestations. If you are up for the challenge, you can attend a film festival, an international dance festival, and visit at least three museums in an eight-hour time frame. Tonight is no exception. I'm attending the show of Bulgarian extreme performer, Ivo Dimchev. From what I've read, Ivo is guaranteed to knock my socks off because quite frankly I've never seen anyone perform something similar. Think of him as a David Bowie meets Bjork at an insane asylum-type persona. Undoubtedly Vienna is where I was supposed to be as my cultural cup runneth over. I soon must start pouring my Viennese influences out into the world. I'm quite eager to witness that which I'll conjure up from this mind-bending Austrian life, once it's all over.

Impregnated with idiosyncrasy, Ivo's performance was by far one of the closest things I've seen to human flirting with otherworldly states of being. Ivo was accompanied by Emilian Gatsov, a Sofia based composer who improvised anything from pillow soft piano keys to ear piercing mechanical sounds from his laptop computer and musical keyboard. As if listening to a variation of hums from a church organ to what resembles the soundtrack of a murder scene in *The Texas Chainsaw Massacre* within a sixty-minute span wasn't enough to make a person bolt out of the room, it was Ivo's suavity to alter from angelic-like states to a full-blown demonic entity that made my eyes bulge and palms sweat. I found myself witnessing a séance gone wrong where a malicious being spoke in tongues and imposed severe convulsions on the unsuspecting and half naked medium. My limited definition of avant-garde performance art was entirely shattered — time to rethink the meaning of pushing the envelope.

July 14, 2012 - Hofburg Imperial Palace

My eyes are not worthy of such beauty. The excessive potency of Europe's longest running and most influential dynasty, the Habsburgs, is architecturally displayed here without limitation. Having been home to some of the greatest leaders in European history, nothing was considered too flamboyant or decadent while constructing this sprawling Baroque style masterpiece. More was definitely more.

Within its walls, this palace-of-palaces has witnessed hundreds if not thousands of imperial balls, and countless concerts by musical titans such as Mozart and Johann Strauss. It's also the winter home to the Spanish Riding School which is the only institution on earth that has practiced and cultivated the fine art of equestrianism for over 440 years in a row. Grotesque amounts of opulence and world defining culture is tossed around here like Frisbees in a dog park.

Conduct the orchestra of your life with grace. Stand on the podium with your conducting baton and feverishly wave it at the ensemble that The Divine has given you to orchestrate. Master all that is you with much finesse.

July 14, 2012

220 plus years after his death we all know the name Wolfgang Amadeus Mozart. Although he was born in Salzburg, Austria he chose Vienna as his home, and composed his finest pieces here. This is a photo of his final

resting place (although some say that the body may not be here). While knowing that Mozart and Johann Strauss were two of its highest profile residents, one would be an incredulous idiot of universal magnitude if they contested Vienna's title as "the City of Music".

I cannot stress enough the power of faith in The Divine. Things may not arrive when you want or as you want them, but keep your faith and one day, sooner or later, you will be gifted with your answers.

July 15, 2012

You can't expect to change your life by doing the same things over and over and hoping for a different result. Change requires exactly that: change. Change of atmosphere, change of mind, change of heart, change of pace, and dare I say change of friends and places you go to. It may be a lonely road at times and you may upset some people along the way but remember that it is your life which is in question. If you want change then change what needs to be changed, move forward and never think about turning back.

July 17, 2012

I've had an epiphany this morning. I realized that I have begun to speak the very basic words in German! I know how to say: "cash register, his, excuse me, please, hello, good-bye, I don't speak German, small, big, chocolate, pistachio, push, and I love Austria!" I say all this with my Miami accent and they still understand — they laugh a little at me — but they understand me!

July 19, 2012

The calendar rolls on by and I'm finding myself even more than I imagined. I'm discovering all that I am. Watering down the hours of the day until they're diluted into nothingness by strolling through the plethora of museums, or bouncing on Julia's bike along the cobblestone streets of this imperial city, has solidified my existence. The more time I spend in Vienna, the more she mirrors all that I love — the louder she echoes my voice.

July 21 - Tribunj, Croatia

I stood on top of the highest hill in Tribunj, Croatia, and elatedly overlooked toward the mountain sprinkled crystal blue Adriatic Sea. I said to myself, "The best thing I could have done with my life was to completely remove all of my fears, listen to my heart, and set sail into this magnificent world." I'm certain in all that I have done.

July 22, 2012

The more one awakens the more one realizes how deeply we as a species have fallen asleep. The more one awakens the more one finds the need to be that alarm clock, to go off on humanity's consciousness, and the more one finds the need to shout, "Wake up, wake up, wake up!"

July 24, 2012

There's an ejection lever to the seat you're on right now. If you don't like where you are sitting at in your life then pull it and blast off. There's very little, if not no guarantee, you'll ever land again; however the thrill of the ride should suffice for an eternity. Pull it, take off, live life as it is intended: free.

July 26, 2012 - Vienna, Austria

The clickety-clack of horses toting tourist stuffed carriages is music to my ears. It serves as a forewarning that within seconds I will visually be teleported to the fascinating days of yesteryear. Vienna's streets are overflowing with these rolling time capsules. Known as "fiakers", these horse-drawn carriages leave nothing to your imagination.

Serenaded in array of colors, the most memorable carriage to date was bright pink with heavy gold accents, and a black hood. In true flamboyant Viennese fashion the fiaker driver wore a long, elegant top hat, and was dressed to the nines in an Old English style black suit with gold buttons. Perched from above, he held a lunge whip in his right hand and graciously used it to hurry-on-up his two powdery white steeds. I was mesmerized by this sight, and noticed that the regal creatures towing the pink cloud of eye candy had their own Viennese flair. They wore perfectly tailored salmon colored earmuffs. Paralyzed in magic, I asked myself, "Did I just see two snow white horses, wearing pink earmuffs, hauling a fuchsia and gold carriage along a cobblestone street?" Immediately I smiled from deep within and said, "You bet, I did." Vienna most certainly delivers.

A love-based mentality leads to a love-based life, and in living a love-based life you become as free as you will ever be in your human form. So let love flow freely through you, let it rein your every thought, your every word and every action. In doing so you will experience the bliss of living life in its highest form because when you operate from 100% pure love the universe immediately acknowledges what it is you're doing and cascades its endless well of supreme goodness into your reality.

JULY 27, 2012

In 3 days my Viennese residency comes to a close. Its finale will seal another chapter on this remarkable journey that Spirit has allowed me to venture on. What did I learn as a Viennese? I understood that Vienna is very much like me because I'm very much like her. I discovered that I have an insatiable appetite and an abysmal love for all of the arts. I've come face-to-face with what I always knew in my heart about myself, but was afraid to tell the world. In my own way, through my writings, my unwillingness to care about others' opinions of me, my street art, my fashion sense, my admiration and profound respect for painters, writers and musicians, my love for the Bohemian life, my unmatched passion for just about anything and everything with color and lights, and my undying perspective that life should be lived to the loudest decibel and the brightest colors, is that I too am an artist. I've realized that my art, just like the possibilities in life, is not limited to just one thing, and that we can be and do anything we want as long as it's fueled with passion and pure intense love. My duties in life have become defined. I must continue bombarding the world's negativity and cynicism using the artillery that I'm heavily equipped with, and that is laughter, art, music, poetry and love.

If this were a game of "hot and cold", now would be the time where I'd hear the words "getting warmer, hot, hotter!" The piece of the ever illusive life puzzle that I've been so diligently scouting for has got to be very close by. I'm familiarizing myself with he, who I am.

July 28, 2012 – Museumsquartier

I invest a few hours a day of almost every day here. Visiting the predominantly concrete courtyard that's encompassed by numerous museums, cafes, and shops has become a wonderful addiction of mine. I enjoy nothing more than lying under the sun on any of the available chunky, red or yellow, plastic lawn chairs set amongst this world renowned cultural mecca. I love coming here and doing absolutely nothing because the energy is constantly fluid; creativity abounds. I sense inspiration by just getting a waft of the air upon entering this quarter. Architecturally it offers both Baroque and modern styles that loosely intermingle with each other as if they were newfound friends drinking heavily at a cocktail party. At times free events are hosted al fresco, offering anything from rousing avant-garde fashion shows under a blanket of stars, to DJs casting lightly thumping beats toward a languorous crowd during the brutal heat of the day. There's always something to whet my creative appetite whenever I repose and soak the energy in.

The light that illuminates your future is powered by your present day thoughts, so think big, bright and clear about the days yet to come and watch how the light that you once thought was only a dim bulb guiding you becomes more powerful than 10,000 suns.

JULY 29, 2012

To The Divine,

Thank you, I'm forever indebted for the marching band of muses you've sent to parade around in my head! I'm grateful for the love, light and clarity you've guided me with. It's because of thee I'm able to become everything I desire to be. I will never cease to proclaim that you're very real, that you're the Almighty, and that you're more powerful than any of the brightest living minds put together can ever fathom. After all it was you who created the universe. Even in what I thought were the starkest of my darkest days you were unraveling a beautiful life lesson. My eyes tear because your love is so immense and eternal, it overpowers me. My mind cannot fully comprehend it. I don't think I can ever thank you enough for the treasures troves you have revealed internally and externally. I'm enrolled as soldier in your army, and I will fight using the world's most powerful weaponry that man will never be able to manufacture, and that is the ceaseless love you have taught me.

People will enter your life who may seem as if all they want to do is stir it up. And that's probably what they've been sent to do. They're Divine messengers of discord yard-sticking the foundations of your temple. The Universe will not build the staircase to its Kingdom on faulty grounds. Do not be shaken by an exterior force. Trust that all is going well no matter how turbulent the storm is. Rest assured the tempest will subside.

Some people choose the safer path in life. They drive on newly paved highways with the nice drivers and all the exit signs clearly marked. I have come to accept that I like to take the dusty backroads with no exit signs, pick up the hitchhikers, make them my friends, and drive through life without ever worrying about which direction I'm heading.

JULY 30, 2012

"Hvala Hvartska" (means "thank you Croatia", and they're the only two Croat words in my vocabulary). As you can imagine, all this traveling leads to plenty of down time in between destinations, and, well you get plenty of opportunities to be silly. On this particular day I was pretending to be a Croat sailor saluting the sun. Imagination and some props go a long way when you're trying to make the most of even the slowest moments.

July 31, 2012

It's hard to believe a month has gone by and the credits are rolling on the Viennese mini-series that was my life here. I've taken my cue from a bleeding sun and begun to pack my things once again. Without a doubt my time in Vienna served me well. I found myself. I discovered that I am an artist, a writer, a poet, a bohemian, a gypsy, a lover of life, and an endless dreamer. I'm a Viennese at heart.

Just as the final hour looms I found that the last piece to one of the life puzzles I've been ever so diligently working on was stuck to the bottom of my shoe the whole time. I just never bothered to look there. I've taken that final puzzle piece off the sole of my foot and placed it right where it belongs. I'm no longer looking at an incomplete life puzzle but a beautiful future instead. My existence makes total sense while yet another lesson is revealed:

At times the answers we are looking for on the exterior are the answers we are already carrying within us. The key to finding them is to make sure we look entirely inside of ourselves before we start to look for them on the outside.

Deep down, I always knew he, who I am: an artist.

CHAPTER 6

Race to the Acropolis

As the money tightens up, I realize that the sands of time belonging to this journey are running against its favor. I look at my diminished bank account and budget; I can probably survive for one or two more months off of the dwindling cash I have left. The life reveal in Vienna did not feel like it was the end. I needed to somehow keep going but stay still at the same time to make my money last.

I decided to head to Budapest where I would be at the gates of Eastern and Southeastern Europe while enjoying a more forgiving currency exchange rate. Now opting for the Hungarian capital as home base, I made an extraordinary sprint toward the tightly wound yellow tape of this journey's finish line. Blasting through both sides of the old Iron Curtain, with the most potent stick of spiritual dynamite in the cosmos, the aftermath leaves beautiful lessons scattered all over Southeastern Europe.

August 1, 2012 – Budapest, Hungary

The red velvet curtain that was draped over the stage of my life as a Budapester has parted: The Hungarian Hector show has begun!

First things first. Let me start by pointing out this fact: The Hungarian language is dreadfully difficult. Just as I was learning how to speak German like a toddler, I moved to Hungary, soon to realize that this is the only country with Latin script, where I can't make out the word "pharmacy" which in Hungarian is gyógyszertár (seriously, who came up with that?). There's a tale about how Hungarians made a lot of words difficult to save themselves from becoming German speakers. After trying to speak German in Austria for a month, I don't blame them; however I don't think they did any better. It seems almost every other word has an accented letter. I read somewhere that on the average every sixth Hungarian letter is accented somehow. Confused? So am I.

Now that you understand that I have embryonic aspirations of ever acquiring any knowledge on anything I listen to or read for the next month, let me share with you why I turned up here. Budapest oozes soul. It gushes with authenticity; it's one of those cities where the visual pollution of the Madison Avenue masterminds is found far, few, and in between. Quaint mom and pop shops set forth your imagination with never-before-seen memorabilia from the Communist era; a vast horde of bakeries reel you in with the seducing scent of Hungarian delicacies, all of which flank the main shopping streets. Its cafés are at par with the upper echelon of those in Paris, yet they're understated and equably priced. Geographically, the city is found at the crossroads of Eastern and Southern Europe and graciously offers economic transport on a train right out of its Keleti Railway Station, allowing one to further peruse the intestines of the Old World. And after visiting 35 + cities, the Hungarian Parliament building in Budapest remains my favorite piece of architecture in the world. Built in Gothic Revival style, no other edifice on the planet is equally as surreal. Budapest, or "BP" as the locals call it, is my beloved August home.

August 5, 2012

The luminous path may not always have light. The secret is in learning how to fearlessly walk in its darkness.

August 5, 2012

I am most afraid of living a life half lived. And to live in fear is no longer an option. That old paradigm has shattered. I have discovered that the more I live doing what I love, the more I understand how precious the gift of life truly is. I have come to the realization that one must seize every moment and every opportunity. With this said I make a proclamation to the city of Cairo that in 17 days I will pour my heart out on its streets, and I vow to my eyes that they will feast on the site of The Great Pyramids of Giza.

August 6, 2012

It is impossible to have a magic show without a magician, and you can't be a magician if you don't believe in magic. Every day life hands us a new cape and wand, and it is our choice to use them or not. Today, like every day, I will choose to be a magician. The availability of magic in our lives isn't a secret; it's meant to be out in the open. Stop participating in someone else's magic show. Pick up your cape and wand, and go cast your own miraculous spells. All the sorcery you need is right inside of you. Abracadabra.

A truly liberated soul cares not one ounce what anyone thinks of it, for it has long broken free from the prison of other's judgments.

August 7, 2012

Imagine that you are six years old and that it's Christmas Eve. You still believe in Santa Clause and the Tooth Fairy. Mickey Mouse is your idol. Also picture that you're in a car with your parents on the way to Disney

World, singing Christmas Carols when all of a sudden a tooth falls out! So now you are expecting Santa Claus, Mickey Mouse *and* the Tooth Fairy in less than 24 hours. You are so excited that your little heart may just pop out of your body and run away screaming madly!

Well, that's a close second to the level of excitement that I'm feeling right now because in my pocket there's a five-day all access pass to Sziget Festival (Sziget Fest currently holds the title to Europe's best major music festival). This all access pass that I hold is valid starting tomorrow. It's safe to say that my notion of sleep has fled the country. The butterflies in my stomach have morphed to a torrent of locusts and my heart is pounding somewhere at about 150 BPMs. The reason I am so excited? The lineup looks like this: The XX, Bebel Gilberto, Snoop Dog, Magnetic Man, Azari & III, Friendly Fires, Saint Ettiene, The Roots, The Killers, Korn, Yonderboi, Lamb, The Ting Tings, Friendly Fires, and much, much more.

AUGUST 8, 2012 – ÓBUDA ISLAND, BUDAPEST, HUNGARY

At the current moment, and for the next five days, there won't be another place on this earth with more musical energy than Óbuda Island! Sziget Festival, has officially begun.

Goocoo from Japan ripped open the main stage at Sziget today. They're seven female and four male Taiko drummers. From the very second they got on the black and red candy cane striped grandstand they commanded the audience to dance spontaneously by feverishly pounding on over 15 Taiko drums.

In the captivity free seconds I had from the magic of Goocoo, I did a quick scan of the area. At 2500 feet behind me was the Sziget Eye, a larger than life Ferris wheel lazily spinning while shielding the hip thrusting crowd of thousands from the midday sun. Next to the swirling wheel was an equally tall blue and white crane elevating a duo of daredevil bungee jumpers to chilling heights. Below the two Goliath-like structures were pockets of puffing smoke bathing the tree framed area. I smelled burgers, pizza, french-fries and other cooked foods.

A 180 degree scope though the beat infected crowd showed that all nations were present. It was evident by the sea of multi-national flags fluttering in the wind (perhaps even dancing) protruding over the masses. From countries as far away as South Africa, to even a pirate flag, no group on the planet was absent. It was all very clear, everyone wanted to experience the hypnotic effects of Gooccoo.

Twenty-five bone shaking, dirt stomping minutes went by and finally the 11 Pied Pipers of Hamelin showed mercy on us by finalizing the show. The fiery swarm of people showed their gratitude to the musical maestros by cheering at eardrum popping levels for over 5 minutes. My hands stung so badly from clapping they felt like I'd picked up a jellyfish. What a stupendous show!

AUGUST 10, 2012

Dear Universe,

Just to make this clear: I am your tumbleweed. So feel free to continue to forcefully howl your cosmic winds my way and keep me rolling through all the magic that is you. I believe.

Today, while attending Sziget, music taught me an invaluable lesson by demonstrating that when it's present it has not one interest in making any kind of judgments. The only thing that music has its sights on is its desire to set us free. Music has always been the answer. We, could all be, like music.

There isn't a better person in the world to make fun of than yourself.

Always shine as bright as you can, even if others cannot withstand. The sun didn't become the brightest star in our galaxy by opaquing its light.

Today I explored Sziget city. Tenderly cradled by the Danube River, the makeshift party town on the sumptuous green island of Obuda lacks absolutely nothing. If you have dreamt it, chances are it has materialized at the festival.

With a population of 35,000 residents pitching tents on the island for a week, it is without wonder why I witnessed endless camping districts hosting different nationalities. Italian, French, and German micro-cities, proudly boasting their respective flags, were in full bloom. The string and cloth civilizations were woven together by the needles of the LGBT, Jewish, Gypsy, and African cultures. It was like visiting the UN, only everyone was in agreement about everything. This was evident by the echoes of laughter, communal barbeques, and embodied by a mid-twenties, punk-rock, Dutch boy, sporting an orange mohawk, holding hands with his younger, barefoot, flower power, Spanish girlfriend. "If only the entire world would choose to live in such harmony," I said to myself.

It would have been satisfying enough to solely experience the cultural fiber of the mega party. But the economic engine that catapults Sizget city was equally as thrilling. A Thai massage tent, a tattoo parlor (at least I think it was festival sponsored), a quirky hairdresser, marriage and travel bureaus, a pharmacy, a place to repair or rent a bicycle, and even a tent offering free hugs. The gastronomical choices were equally as diverse as its populace; Balkan, Indian, Arab, Chinese, and Thai.

Entertainment was not left to just the musicians. On the quieter part of the island I discovered a Hungarian village offering traditional games such as stilt walking, and live folk music shows inside a barn. Random street performers magically appeared along the oak tree lined walkways. One moment I was pummeled by the sounds of a 20 piece Brazilian bateria stomping down a dirt path, and the next I was encircled by the chaos of a full-blown, time-honored, Chinese wedding procession. Without a chance to blink I found myself at the gates of a socialist era circus.

The commie fantasyland left no detail absent. At the entrance I was asked to fill out paperwork for admittance. A passport was required to proceed.

After all I was stepping into a different time. Back then no one could leave their home without their documents, much less go to the circus without proper identification. With a passport in hand, I was interrogated for five minutes by a blank-faced, female officer before I was allowed beyond the second checkpoint. Once inside I discovered all sorts of games, zero of which I had ever played. Periodically, strolling guards would stop and ask me for my passport. For a while it all felt so real.

I can always count on her voice to sing to me during the times of my chosen loneliness. She croons the melodies of the innocent prisoners, the hungry children, the forgotten, the plagued, and that of the many others who are less fortunate than I. She hums these chants in my ear just before bed to remind me of how blessed I have always been. She is the muse that lives inside my head.

AUGUST 11, 2012

Lately there's been a lot of press on these inspiring boards that have popped up all over the world. They are designed to allow you to write in the things you want to do before you take in your last breath. Here's a small portion of the ever-changing, freight container sized piece of artwork located right by the World Stage at the Sizget Music Festival. My favorite fill-in was the one where the person put their phone number! Basically they said, "Hey world, call me." My fill-in said, "Before I die, I want to inspire the world", and that I intend to do.

August 12, 2012

Dancing in a circle pit while Anti-Flag's rock music blares from a stage caged with gargantuan speakers can be scratched off my bucket list! Ironically the song that lured me to the dusty ring of free shoves and flying fists was *Broken Bones*. Albeit I didn't crush any part of my body, I did take an elbow to the face. The price was well worth it, the experience was exhilarating! Why did I take so long to fall in love with Rock n Roll?

Allow yourself to become a bastion of glory and ALL that is good. Become an impenetrable fortress where evil and negativity have no chances of breaking into your peace.

The line between your dreams and reality is drawn by faith and commitment. The more you commit and the stronger your faith the thinner the line becomes.

August 13, 2012

Sziget Fest 2012 sadly ends but Hungary should be proud of its accomplishments. More so, Budapest, the city that beautifully frames this spectacle, should stand high and mighty with its chin up, as Sziget Fest is fighting in the heavily contested battlegrounds for the heart and soul of Europe's music festivals, and is winning! Rightfully it has earned the title of Europe's best major music festival.

I woke up today to find that the electricity of the Sziget Fest is still very much running through my veins. I need to keep that energy flowing. I've decided to catch a last minute train to Belgrade, Serbia.

With a price tag equivalent to $13 and after reading all the reviews about shady characters, filth, rude employees, frequent stops, and security checks, I eagerly bought my ticket on the overnight train to Serbia. It leaves in less than two hours.

Sure I will have to sleep with one eye open, and I will probably catch some pulmonary infection from breathing the air inside notoriously filth ridden compartments, but these are the kind of experiences that I draw inspiration from, and find "fun". Secretly (not so secret anymore) I'm hoping there's an internationally wanted criminal on board, that the Interpol raids my train, and catches him/her due my heroic actions of some sort. I know it's a far-fetched thought, but a guy can always dream.

AUGUST 14, 2012 – BELGRADE, SERBIA

I survived the night train from Budapest to Belgrade. Yes, there were a few questionable characters on board (including a babbling drunk wearing an eye patch) but considering I was riding through the Hungarian and Serbian countryside at unholy hours of the night, it was more than expected. I flirted with sleep for the most part of the eight-hour adventure but couldn't manage to seduce it. When the train was brought to a halt at an eerie Serbian border town around 3AM for passport control, I was wide awake.

Even though I am the owner of a highly coveted American passport, international crossings over land always make me apprehensive. There's something very unnerving about being on the boundary line of two countries I know nothing about. Naturally, when the rotund, milky skinned armed guard poked me on the shoulder requesting "dohcooment", I was a little jumpy.

Anticipating the moment I quickly pulled out my travel documents from a brimming bookbag and handed them to him. After scanning my passport with a handheld device, he scoped me up and down with piercing eyes, looked at the picture on my travel permit and deemed me worthy of entering his country by stamping it with an authorization to proceed. With a neutral stare on his face, he proclaims: "Velcome to Serrrbia".

Upon exiting Belgrade's central rail station at 7AM, it hit me: I was in the nerve core of Eastern Europe. No longer were there any signs of American influence whatsoever: No Coca-Cola bottles on display for sale, no golden arches with free wifi nearby, and no smiling faces to be found anywhere. There was nothing I could relate to. I cautiously headed to my hotel and realized that I was in the capital city of the old Yugoslavia, and recalled the NATO bombings that occurred here during the Kosovo War in the late nineties.

After dropping off my tiny and bursting-at-the-seams bag at a mediocre inn, where I only chose to stay for proximity to the train station and low-low cost, I dared to explore Belgrade. Its streets were the closest I had ever come to a recent war. The burnt shells of bombed-out buildings still remained and I presumed were left as memories of a traumatizing era no one ever wants to relive again. Outside of the war-torn pockets, Belgrade offered a glimmer of hope with a bustling, historic center filled with cafés and up and coming Serbian shops of all kinds. There is also a prolific street art movement which is a clear indicator that Serbian youth have embraced the outside world it was once deprived of.

Entertain your mind with pure thoughts, otherwise your mind will entertain you with everything but.

When trying to accomplish a dream, never get caught up in the logistical factors of how things will happen because you are not in control of them. Simply eradicate doubt and negativity. Keep your mind solely on what you want to achieve. See yourself having or doing it. Practice positive thinking and speaking. Watch how your dream unfolds.

I'm going to exert myself further out of my comfort zone and continue "trucking" through Southeastern Europe. Tomorrow morning I'm hopping on a ten-hour train ride to Skopje, Macedonia. Why Macedonia? Because there is a captivating nation bordering just south of it, and that alluring nation is the same country that birthed civilization as we know it. I always dreamt of seeing the Acropolis in Greece and while knowing that I'm heading for the home stretch of this journey, and I will wrap it up in the next month and a half or so, I intend on ending it with as much passion and vigor as it started. The race to the Acropolis has begun.

For the past few months I haven't been able to decipher if the word looping from a song I keep playing over and over using my iPod is "faith" or "fate". I mean after all it's hard to tell what a subtle voice is saying amidst some pretty slamming Deep House beats. The meek voice is found hiccupping the one word in between the kick drum and the clap, and if you are not paying attention you may miss it altogether. However I sensed that something had drawn me to listen closely. Because of this I have been religiously asking myself, "What is she saying? Is it faith or is it fate?" for over four months now. Then it hit me out of "nowhere" as it usually does when one seeks unconventional universal wisdom. The female voice is saying both "fate" and "faith". She has been the voice of universal guidance telling me to have FAITH in my FATE. Her words were perfectly situated in what may have been perceived as the most outlandish of places by a conventional thinker. Luckily I don't do conventional anything these days, and because of this I found the answer that I needed to "hear" today:

Have faith in your fate Hector, keep on going.

AUGUST 15, 2012 – ON A TRAIN BETWEEN SERBIA AND MACEDONIA

Out of all the whimsical European railroad journeys I have ventured on in my life, none have offered such a unique combination of grit, magic, cultural divulgence and extreme natural beauty as this one. When I first walked into the misty railway station at the crack of dawn there were a scant amount of trains waiting to depart. I scanned the mostly desolate area but no train looked entirely "operable". They were heavily vandalized, short in length, and dated back to at least the 1960s. There was a particular one on track number 2 that was the most alarming.

It was the shortest I've ever seen with only three rail cars, all of which were multicolored, both from heavy graffiti and extreme oxidation. Doubting that my ride was present, I looked at my yellowish ticket stub to confirm my train's railway number: There it was, track number 2 clearly stated on my travel pass. For a second I hesitated to enter, but quickly realized I needed to jump on, and make my way to Skopje —after all, this mission was about getting to the Acropolis, not riding on only nice trains. My seat had been assigned: cabin number 36, chair number 3.

Since the span of the train was so short I immediately found my cabin. To my utmost amusement I discovered that I'd be sharing it with a garishly dressed gypsy family of four. The father in his early 40s, had a deeply cracked and sun worn face. He chain smoked cigarettes of an unidentifiable brand in saggy light blue jeans, and badly scuffed white sneakers. He was the most "Western looking" one out of all of them. The mother and two young daughters were ripped right out of a page from a *National Geographic Magazine*.

They wore tightly wrapped, satin like, floral print headscarves that concealed most of their jet black hair. Their thick and bushy eyebrows were complemented by the dark olive hue of their skin. The mother, also an avid smoker, was in her early 30s. The daughters were between 6 and 8 years old. All three were in dresses so drunken in colors they'd make any sparkling rainbow look sober. I noticed that the entire family was humbly toting worn-out plastic bags, stuffed with loaves of bread, cheese, canned foods, toilet paper, and soiled clothing.

We made our way into the serenity of the Serbian countryside and the scenery grew increasingly beautiful. We zipped by picturesque villages set at the foothills of steep mountain ranges. Our "little engine that could" tugged with all its might and lead us through jaw-dropping ravines adorned with long forgotten medieval castles. I spent countless hours gazing into this sublimity. I was so entranced by natural beauty, I did not care that there was no air conditioning on this train despite the record breaking heat.

Before reaching the Macedonian border, the colorful family made an exit at small town where we had stopped. Just as they were leaving, the younger of the two daughters offered me a piece of bread from one of the dilapidated plastic bags she was carrying. We never verbally communicated but the simple gesture of her feeble arm extended toward me with balmy hands clasping a meager bag with days-old bread inside of it, said more than 1000 words could ever say. I thought, *Materially she has nothing yet spiritually she has everything.* Instantly Mathew 5:5 comes to mind: "The meek shall inherit the earth."

Without a chance to blink, a thin, handsome young man with the aura of an angel approached me. He spoke perfect English: "Excuse me, what time is it?"

My ears welcomed this inflection of language as they finally savored a familiar sound. I dug for my iPhone, then responded, "It's 1:00 PM." After thanking me, our conversation continued. His name was Vagelis. He told me that he was on his way home from Ozora Fest in Hungary. The festival is a psychedelic tribal gathering held in the Hungarian countryside, and it attracts free spirits from all over Europe.

I asked him, "Where's home?" He told me he's from Athens. As the "ah" sound from Athens came out of his mouth my heart accelerated, and I was overcome with a sense of relief because technically I wasn't sure of how to get to Athens once I arrived to Skopje. *He's an angel who was sent to guide me,* I thought. He was confident that we're best of buddies, and made a confession after pulling out a pair of orange grip pliers from his pocket. "I am using these to break into the small mechanical room every time the train stops at a station."

Not very angel-like, I thought, so I asked, "Why are you doing that?"

His response was that he'd spent all his money at Ozora, and now he must stowaway to get home.

I invited him to have a seat in my cabin, feeling sure no one would claim the tottering chairs inside since they were recently vacated. He restlessly accepted but only stayed for a few minutes, then got up to talk to some stragglers down the hall and vanished.

I focused on the distinct clatter of the railway, and drifted into a dreamless sleep with its uninterrupted swinging, and Rock-a-bye Baby humming *thump-thump-thump-thump.*

The train made a stop at the next town and I was awakened by the brusque sound of guards yelling. I didn't understand a word they were saying, but their intonation lead me to believe they were quite upset. I looked out the window and saw two elephantine men wrestling Vagelis and the duo of scruffy stragglers off the train. They roughly chucked their helpless bags onto the gravel, making a crunching sound. A sharp whistle blew and the train sluggishly departed. *There goes my guardian angel,* slowly seeping into the very depths of my overtaxed vision.

AUGUST 15, 2012 - SKOPJE, MACEDONIA

Skopje was unlike any European city I have ever visited. Its train station not only lacked a tremendous amount of charm, it was bereft of any kind of hygiene. The men's bathroom had no toilets, just holes in the floor. The makeshift mirror was all but a cracked quarter of a whole one, resting on a wall layered in dirty fingerprints, and decorated with hand-sketched phallic objects. The filthy handprint motif was a recurring theme throughout the entire train station.

I did not want to stay a second more in this Eden of gunk. I walked outside to get my bearings. To my surprise, the contrast between Skopje and any other major city I've been to so far, was drawn further. The "central" station was in the middle of nowhere. Set smack in the bull's-eye of two desolate streets, I looked at an empty field of burnt grass just across the way. In the far distance was a scant amount of beaten down residential buildings – depression loomed. I was not sure where to go or even what to do. I had assumed I'd be left in the city center. I checked for a Wifi signal using my phone but none were available. In a desperate attempt to figure out where the nerve core of this town was I made the mistake of talking to a group of sketchy cab drivers lurking just outside the station like a pack of starving hyenas. I spoke in English, but none of them knew exactly what I was saying. However they portrayed interest in my words by leaning in. Then I heard a heavily accented voice, deeply bathed in baritone: "I can help you."

I looked up, and the bass was echoing from the mouth of a much taller, and rough looking man. He had strong ethnic features that were indicative of the area; olive skin, bushy eyebrows, and penetrating eyes. He was in his late 40s; I could tell by the grays and blacks that were equally disbursed on his unshaven and timeworn face. I asked for help, telling him I needed to find a safe place to sleep, before the now disappearing sun entirely set.

Puffing on a cigarette, he said he knew of a hostel where I could sleep, and that the fare to get there would be 10 Euros, a hefty price to pay for such a depressed country. Against every instinct, I hopped in his rusty, white 1983 Toyota Corolla. The seats were deteriorated; cracked by the sun, they scratched the sweaty palms of my hands.

We headed in a direction that took us farther and farther away from the "center". Thirty minutes went by and he made a quick turn into a gangster's paradise. A hundred thoughts flashed through my mind, none of which had anything to do with feeling secure. The deluge of horrifying mental images was paused by the sound of squeaking brakes and the rocking of the car brought to a sudden stop. The driver seemed to be asking a rough looking group of teenage boys for directions.

The horror reel in my mind spun once again. *That's it, this is the end,* I thought. *They are going to murder me.* Panic stricken, I demanded the driver return me to the train station. There was no way in hell I was staying here.

The driver questioned my reasoning, but didn't try to convince me otherwise. The language barrier between us made things all the more difficult. He probably wouldn't earn the commission from whatever shack he intended on having me stay at. Disappointment seeped from his coffee stained white T-shirt as we made our way back to square one.

What do I do now? was the first question that came to mind when I was dropped off at the creepy railway station. Dusk had long passed and in a frenzied state, I looked for a "sign" everywhere. *The universe has got to give me some sort of clue, I need help,* and as the final word disappeared from thought, I heard my name ardently called: "Hector, Hector, Hector!" It was Vagelis yelling to get my attention! The guardian angel I knew him to be arrived at the very moment I needed him most. Having found his way to Skopje by hitchhiking and accepting donations from strangers for bus fare he told he knew how to make our way to Athens. "We must sleep in the station tonight and take the 6:00 AM bus across the border to Thessaloniki, Greece. From Thessaloniki we must take a seven hour train ride to Athens. Don't worry about a single thing, I know how to get us there." And just like that, he siphoned all the fear out of my body and replaced it with equanimity.

Now in a state of serenity I thought about how all this happened. There was nothing "chance" about this encounter with Vagelis. This was the work of the Universe. It's what's known as synchronicity.

"Synchronicity is the experience of two or more events that are apparently causally unrelated or unlikely to occur together by chance, yet are experienced as occurring together in a meaningful manner." - Wikipedia

The Universe is constantly noosing what may seem to be unrelated events, and hands them to us for an opportunity to experience growth, teach us a lesson, lead us down the right path, and find our destinies. These seemingly uncorrelated experiences are boundless, meaning that the Universe never stops placing them in our paths. The more in tune we become with "coincidences", and figure out how to decipher them, the easier life will flow. This isn't philosophy, it's what governs growth and creation in the astros. Think about it on the simplest level: If there wasn't such a thing as synchronicity, how would flowers be pollinated by the bees and birds? If you think about it on a deeper level, you will realize that everything around us is governed by this incorruptible truth.

Some may say: "But wait, that's too many coincidences," and I will agree. The mind will never be able to understand the magnitude of the supreme grandiosity that we are a part of. The trick is not to over-think things, and trust that the same source that keeps this giant rock in the middle of space perfectly spinning in its orbit is the same source that is divinely orchestrating the events of our lives.

Trust in it, and you will be set free of all your worries.

The shiniest toy isn't always the one that's the most fun to play with.

One thing I've learned is that life is just a series of ever-changing moments. We have good ones and bad ones, rich ones and poor ones, weird ones, scary ones, confusing ones, doubtful and certain ones. The list goes on and on and on. The key to being able to maintain your calm or cool throughout any of the many "ONES" is to not grow attached to them, recall the law of impermanence. Understand that you can't always be happy and you won't always be sad but you will always have peace available to you if you choose to seek it. This is truth, and a governing spiritual law in my book, because I found peace to be the place where our soul lives. I have found that once you turn your attention to the eternal safe haven of serenity that lives inside, you will no longer overreact to situations that shake you, and you will not grow attached to a passing moment of joy.

Devour moments of happiness like a lion does a bloody carcass. Know that the "happy moment" will fill you, but not forever. Understand that you will grow hungry again, enjoy the present meal.

AUGUST 16, 2012 – ATHENS, GREECE

It is the fate of every archaic soul to make its return to Athens.

With a history spanning over 3400 years, I'm convinced that the Greek capital was an old haunt of my being. The ancient city resurrects that feeling of a familiar unfamiliarity—I've been here before yet I haven't. Athena, as the Greeks refer to the city, is the birthplace of democracy; and the ancient cobbled grounds I walk on are the same ones that inspired philosophical behemoths such as Aristotle and his teacher Plato. Somehow I'm able to trace the energetic vestige of all the brilliant minds who've stepped on the same cracks. For me, the sidewalks of Athens are living libraries overflowing with volumes of intellectual inspiration. I sense the intense presence of superior thought form in the air.

The city is crowned by a Unesco World Heritage site known as the Acropolis. The highlight structure of the Acropolis is the Parthenon which is a religious monument built in Classical Greek style as a temple to Athena (who the city is named after) the goddess of civilization as we know it. The whole of the Acropolis rests on a flat top rock 490 feet in the air, making the jaw-dropping ruins visible from almost anywhere in the city.

Can't wait to go to bed tonight, not for the fact that I will finally get some rest, or the hope of waking to the memory of a beautiful dream. Instead, the excitement is about the idea that when I wake up tomorrow it will be the day I ascend on the steps of the Acropolis. Just after the passing of tonight's moon I will have succeeded in lassoing yet another dream. This and only this is why I desire sleep.

AUGUST 17, 2012 – ACROPOLIS, ATHENS, GREECE

As I made my way up the sacred rock, toward the mystic ruins that seduced me from hundreds of miles away, my heart pounced against the walls of my chest as if it were banging on a locked exit door of a flaming house. I knew I had arrived at a powerful site. At 2500 years of age this is a lasting testament to the Golden Age of Greece. And by no means is it anywhere near the top of any modern day pilgrim's list of scared sites, yet I was drawn here.

This was once the center of rituals and ceremonies of a highly evolved civilization, and I could sense it. Perhaps long forgotten by most I was haunted by the ghosts of pilgrims from Greece's yesteryear. I could hear their reverent prayers to Athena asking her to deliver the city from evil. I heard the sounds of crumbling rocks underneath their timeworn sandals as they marched up this same path. I sensed their thirst from a scorching summer sun yet I had just drunk water. My ankles jiggled. Was this all a memory of a past life? Could I have jumped in and out of another timeline? These questions provided an even more eerie experience.

In a flash the echoes of the past dissipated and I returned to present time. There I was amongst hundreds of smiling tourists from all nations taking snapshots of the ruins. I too, took out my camera and smiled. I headed for the most picturesque of spots for a photo. I wondered had anyone else felt what I had just experienced.

In the last couple of days I've daringly crossed through four international borders (Hungary, Serbia, Macedonia, and Greece). I've been in every possible emotional spectrum a human being can experience. I have felt the unmistakable vibration of laughter in my tummy, and have savored the salt of warm tears running down my face exuded by fright, and yet uncovered another heirloom in the shape of a lesson: The human being can endure and adapt to just about anything. We are creatures designed for survival, and when we are willing to go after what we want, we'll go through anything to get it. Today the race to the Acropolis has gloriously concluded. I am the winner.

August 18, 2012

The only thing that's able to bind me these days is gravity. Don't be mistaken, the glorious vagabond life is not easy. If it were a simple task then everyone would be living it. This life comes with much sacrifice, and in order to experience it I had to renounce fear and insecurity. I threw in all my poker chips with zero fright of losing everything. I conquered the cowardice of solitude, and lived in absolute silence. I deposited my entire trust in what I couldn't see, hear or touch, and unconditionally believed that a divine source lived internally. I learned how to seek my truths in the howls of the wind. I banked on a system called faith and utilized a limitless debit card funded by the universal wisdom that lives in the heart. I also learned that there are no written rules and the only light that illuminated my path was the one I created for myself. Faith is everything.

The luxury of youth is an advantage that will not always belong to me. Therefore I find it wise to use it as much as I can by intensely living and loving every second that I possess it. I will not die with an unfulfilled wish in my heart.

August 19, 2012 – Athinaikon Hotel Athens, Greece

It is 3:56 AM. I can't sleep in this rickety bed, but the twelve dollar a night accommodation has nothing to do with it. I am still very much on a natural high having just returned from hours of buzzing and weaving through this compelling city on a motorbike driven by Vagelis. Not only did he save my life by helping me make my way here when I was astray in Macedonia, but he has also become an invaluable source of information on Greek life. He has shared details on how the economical situation in Greece has a chokehold on the country's morale, and how he doesn't foresee much of a future for himself here. He confesses that it's virtually impossible for him to acquire financing to go to school with a government that is bankrupt. Additionally, his prospects for work are grim having been recently laid off from a coveted job repairing Italian made coffee machines. There's seemingly no future for him yet his smile is immoveable. There's a glimmer of hope in his eyes because he fervently lives in the moment. He understands something that most people don't, and that is the unabridged power found by living in the very essence of the *now*.

AUGUST 20, 2012

It has been a while since a hero has crossed my path, or perhaps it's been some time since one moved me as much as this boy did. I'm guessing he's about 8 years old. He plays the accordion on the streets of Athens for money. His English was perfect, his accordion skills were on point, and his manners were flawless. I gave him one Euro for him to play any song of his choice, and he was more than delighted in doing so. After I walked away from him, I couldn't help but shed a few tears and feel gratitude for the life that I've had (once again). He becomes the fifth hero of my journey.

August 21, 2012

The sands of time in Athens are quickly drawing to an end. With its finale I pen the last chapters of the story that has been this massive journey around Planet Earth. Just like in any grand literary work I'm going to ensure that the last pages of my story are mind-blowing.

A few weeks ago I posed the question: "What is a trip around the world without setting foot on African soil?" The obvious answer surfaced. After a few clues from the Universe that included my iPod accidentally looping on a song I never knew I owned, which said: "Egypt, Egypt, Egypt" shortly after I asked the question about visiting the land of the Sahara, I decoded the "sign" from the cosmos, booked a flight and I will be on my way to Africa in three days.

In the meantime I intend on making my last hours in Athens memorable ones. They will include dinner with Vagelis's family, aimlessly strolling around the streets, and catching the last glimpses of the Acropolis before it enters my memory bank.

Unhappiness is birthed in the wombs of worry.

Athens may be burning but the smoke from it's fire is all I desire to breathe.

Just like the universes have no end, the depths of our souls have no bottom. We are limitless creatures who have only begun to explore the endless oceans of possibility inside us.

We've undergone the Industrial and Technological Revolution, and yet we are still seeking happiness. This is why the spiritual insurrection is occurring. It's a quiet and seemingly nonexistent one, but it's surely happening and our generation is pioneering it. Never before have we as a species been so collectively open to the power of spirituality. Never in our entire human history have we been so accepting to the belief of life on other planets, of multiple dimensions outside of our immediate perspective, of an innumerable amount of galaxies, and of The Divinity that orchestrates it all.

We will never win the bloodless war we're fighting against time. It's best that we burn down the gates to all that inhibits us. Riot against unhappiness; bombard the hatred and ignorance that may live inside of us with endless missiles of love. Fortify our inner peace and never bunker down love, for time will one day conquer the city that is us.

CHAPTER 7

Arch de Triomphe

E very victory deserves a commemoration. Having found my true self and convinced that I was triumphant in the battle against the demons that taunted me for a decade, I planned my celebration in the only city in the world where such a huge win could be reveled: Paris. However before I arrived at the City of Light, I still had a date with destiny in the desserts of North Africa. The longing to touch Egyptian soil came from deep within me. I needed to lasso that last wild horse. If this adventure was a reconnect with the terra firma of past lives then the bewitching land of gravity defying obelisks, caches of mummies, Tutankhamun, The Great Sphinx, and Ra was the birthplace of my soul's many incarnations on this earth. I desperately needed to go back.

August 21, 2012 - Budapest, Hungary

I'm back at my temporary home base, but just for a few hours. I've only returned to pick up some fresh clothing I left in my monthly rental, and to prepare for tomorrow. With solely twenty-four hours left to reach the Pyramids of Giza I recalled saying goodbye to Miami, and not having a single intention of placing foot on Egyptian soil. However I had zero set commitments. The only vows I made were to subject my ears to the calling of my heart and learn to dance to the rhythm-of-the-music that is life. For the past 2,568 hours or so, that is exactly what I've done. And in doing such a "mad" thing I've found the Shangri-La of Shangri-La's: serenity while seeing the world. As I mentioned earlier: just as the physical miles journeyed have been colossal so have been the spiritual miles I've seized. I've downright submerged myself thousands-upon-thousands of leagues into the depths of the soul and found that my spiritual submarine cannot reach bottom because it is boundless. It has no end. What I have been able to do on these abysmal excursions is pick up invaluable life lessons, return to the surface and share them. Now the song of life has raised its volume to the loudest of decibels, leading my dancing heart toward the deserts of North Africa. All the while, the morale of the crew that runs my soul's submarine is at an all time high — they're ready to take the plunge and pervade even deeper.

August 22, 2012 - Cairo, Egypt

I'll never have to imagine the elation felt by attending 1000 simultaneous wedding parties because I've witnessed them on the streets of the Egyptian megalopolis. Having arrived just after the end of the holy month on the Muslim calendar known as Ramadan, Cairo, a city tallied with a population of over nine million, was in total jubilee. There I was, delightfully confused in an ocean of an ecstatic populace who survived the last 30 days without drinking alcohol, refraining from sexual relations, cursing, in most cases not smoking, and severe fasting.

The deafening thunder of M-80s intermittently launched from the tiny hands of cackling boys was a close second to that of the blaring sound systems off the armada of party boats thumping Chaabi music along the Nile River. Bursting at the seams with dancing passengers, these floating Christmas trees provided visual overstimulation with their dizzying light shows. Back on the streets there were outbursts of wedding parties at every turn. Brides decked out in all sorts of brightly colored wedding dresses, gleefully posed for pictures with friends and strangers alike. Traffic was at a complete standstill but that didn't stop those mounted on gaunt horses from galloping in between hooting cars. I also caught a glimpse of a confused camel, draped in colorful garbs, hauling pink skinned tourists, dressed as if they were on an African safari. Chatty food vendors stood behind poorly lit and sizzling stalls. They were jam-packed along the deeply cracked and sand filled sidewalks selling an array of local delicacies, none of which were familiar to me.

There are no written words or photographs that can transmute the enveloping magic that is Cairo more so the marvel of the energy one senses in Egypt, the almighty queen of Africa.

AUGUST 23, 2012 - THE MUSEUM OF EGYPTIAN ANTIQUITIES

Walking amongst the spine-chilling relics of a civilization that is 5000 years old rattled the deepest levels of my inner being. It's impossible to fully comprehend that people like you and I were living so long ago. I couldn't help but wonder where are those archaic souls at that very moment in time? More so it made me question where would my soul be 5000 years in the future?

These thoughts were so overwhelmingly piercing they moved me to tears. Petrified at the realization of this truth, I pulled myself off to the side where no one could see me sobbing. Seconds later, as if an angel had shot down from the heavens parting the skies to console me, I was overtaken with a sense of calm and cool. "There is no beginning because there is no end," I said to myself. "Time is an illusion of the mind; a fantasy that is only a reality on Planet Earth. The soul knows not a single thing about seconds, hours, days and years. It is unlimited and infinite in its existence. It is indestructible. It is not of the earth. There is no reason to fear death." Sensing a tremendous amount of consolation from seemingly out of nowhere, I felt no need to go on strolling through the haunting antiquities. I quickly made my way to the exit where I found a café to pause in retrospect on this almighty revelation.

There comes a point when you have cast so much light out into the world that darkness has no way of manifesting itself around you.

Burn the bridges to an unnecessary past. Set them ablaze, run away and never look back.

If you are going to light a spiritual fire, only do so in the dessert. Set if off hundreds of miles away from the nearest town or water. In this barren setting your flames can burn uncontrollably for as long as you keep fanning them with the winds of spiritual knowledge. By the time anyone notices what you've done it will be too late for them to do anything about it. They will either run away or be engulfed by your flames of goodness. If they're willing to risk stepping into your inferno of light my advice is to keep them around forever.

AUGUST 24, 2012

Smile with the power of 10,000 suns, it will leave no room for darkness anywhere in the universe.

August 24, 2012 – Pyramids of Giza, Giza, Egypt

Collectively as a species we will die wishing we would have, should have, could have done more in our lives when we had the chance. I personally have refused to be a contributor to this collective thought. This is why I have chosen to live and love, as much as, if today was my last day on this earth. Carrying this belief with a pure conviction in my heart lead me to jump off a camel's back, right in front of the Pyramids of Giza, 6500 miles away from home. I could not be any freer in my human form.

I've grown accustomed to passing a metal detector every time I enter my hotel. I also managed getting used to seeing bomb sniffing dogs randomly circling cars in Cairo traffic, and I also got over the fact that almost everywhere you go there are men packing massive heat, some of them teenagers. I'm not talking about the kind of guns you use one hand to shoot a person with either. I'm speaking about the kind of guns Rambo and Scarface would kill to own. But this is not about seeing weapons on the streets and being constantly under a bomb threat because I kind of expected that. What I didn't expect came from a plastic bottle.

Parched from the unholy desert heat, I bought a large bottle of water while walking along the river Nile (I would tell you how many liters but I could not decipher what was on it). I indulged in the drink, and even though I chugged and chugged, relieving my desert thirst, I didn't entirely finish it. Naively, I kept strolling along the river banks, with the bottle held in plain site (in my right hand). Men yelled at me. I didn't bother paying attention to them because I thought they were one of the many touters coercing me to buy something from the one billion bazaars in this city. Already apprehensive, I continued walking but they kept taunting me. After a few more shouts to the face I finally made eye contact with one of bullies and read his hand gestures (he raised his hand to the head as if holding a glass). He was asking for me to share my water! Turns out, in Egypt it's quite alright to share your bottle of H2O with anyone on the street who asks for some.

Like a true alchemist I transmuted this scenario into a life lesson faster than I can download an app: One must share what they have, and not just only with our immediate family. One must share with our human family as well. Immediately I recall the lesson of Fijian philosophy, we are all one.

If only we all could only de-mummify ourselves from the bandages of society that seeks cheap fame, gathers worthless fortune and consumes without thought.

AUGUST 25, 2012

When walking through the deserts of life we are always presented with mirages. These false illusions of water in our desert come in many forms; but the biggest smokescreen of them all comes in the form of people with faulty promises and broken words. It's like the more you walk toward them the thirstier and the more tired your soul grows but you keep walking in hopes of reaching this oasis they have drawn you to believe exists. Now despite the overwhelming heat you continue walking in this desert of lies believing that their word will lead you to the waters of life. Then at some point you become weary, your soul becomes frail, thin and tired, and you realize that the entire time you have been walking you were walking toward nothing.

At that point you find yourself in one hell of a situation because you are in the middle of this desert with no water, no illusion to follow and nowhere to go. You want to scream because you were so sure you were being led to water by this person. Shortly after this realization you remember your faith and the path that you have walked. You realize that the mirage was set up by The Divine to force you to walk in this desert because it is where you needed to walk through to learn your lesson. At the end of it all you find yourself teary eyed looking up at the sky and laugh because you know eventually the rain will come to alleviate all your thirst.

AUGUST 25, 2012 – PHARAOHS DOKI HOTEL CAIRO, EGYPT

I have been told by my newfound friend and trusted taxi driver, Hany Ahmed, that my hotel happens to be the hot spot for Libyans and Syrians who come to Egypt escaping the recent turmoil in their countries. They stay here until they can find a permanent place in Cairo. Because of this I am particularly fond of all the happenings here. For instance, there are men wearing turbans and robes, chain smoking cigarettes while chatting in the lobby at all hours of the day. Some of them have beat-up briefcases with them and they look like they were really important figures back in their countries. On the first night that I saw this it freaked me out because they were all sizing me up while I was checking in. They were wondering who the Westerner was. Although I was crap in the pants nervous, I stared back at them hard and showed no signs of fear. On the next morning the looks softened up. They were getting used to my Western visage.

Now three days have gone by and we all smile at each other. I've even made a new friend. His name is Haram. He is from Tripoli, Libya and borders 30 years of age. Our conversations go no further than a handshake and a hello but it's reassuring to know that I am now accepted as part of the Libyan and Syrian immigrant crew building a new life in Egypt.

AUGUST 27, 2012 – BUDAPEST, HUNGARY

Once more I've returned to my temporary base. This time it's solely for the purpose to pack all my belongings and depart with no intention of coming back. My thirty-day lease is up and the timing couldn't be any better. The September sky has always been of significance in my life; a rite of passage. The ninth month ushers in a new year of my existence. Also September marks the change of seasons, heralding a shift in climate. With a harvest moon in reach, I sense change, not only in the dying notes of summer's song, but inside of me. I feel closure. I'm ready to lead this journey to its last sun and allow the new season of my life to commence. However I'm ardent on the fact that I must bring this quest to its finale by sealing it with a golden broche. I'm also very much into symbolism and I couldn't think of a more beautifully grand and symbolic city to end this journey other than Paris. The French capital will mark the end of a chapter in my life while mothering a whole new era.

AUGUST 28, 2012

Faith is a supreme power that every man and woman possesses. With it he or she can conquer just about anything. Without it, one is like a boat without water.

After four months of traversing Planet Earth, on the profoundest soul searching mission I've ever been, I've encountered the state of equanimity. I discovered that I'm this at times crazy and artistically inclined, passionate mad man who is desperately seeking to pour out his heart into the world because I'm possessed with insurmountable amounts of creativity and love to give to it. I'm a perpetual dreamer and a ceaseless believer of all that is good. I'm a helpless romantic and I believe that fairy tales do indeed come true. I found that I am a man who wakes up everyday and smiles at the world because he truly understands how precious and fragile life is. I no longer find a need to complain about anything because I've seen people who are living in war-torn nations with deplorable standards of living; who are suffering from hunger, poverty, blindness and just about anything else equally if not more abhorrent, and they manage to smile and complain little if not at all. Lest we forget.

Additionally I've become a man of transparency. I hide nothing from the world because I found that in doing so, the world hides nothing from me. It's like that thick, dusty, heavy black velvet curtain that was draped over everything in my life has been replaced with a thin layer of white onion paper that I can easily poke through with my fingers and see things for what they really are.

Finally, I discovered the light of living in sobriety, and never do I want it to go dark. In the past this would have been one of the harder realities for me to confront as I used to tread lightly on issues that would have drawn me into the line of fire. Now I can proudly stand at the crosshairs of all the misjudgenment, gossip and hearsay that this statement may cause and annihilate it with the utmost powerful weapon we human beings carry, and that is to openly speak the truth.

The truth is I poisoned myself with drugs and alcohol for way too long because I had zero control over them. I had not known true love for self, much less did I understand the sobering power of Spirit. Luckily I escaped that pestilence with life and never did I physically hurt or injure anyone. I must revel in this triumph, relish in this victory, commend this conquest, and Paris awaits.

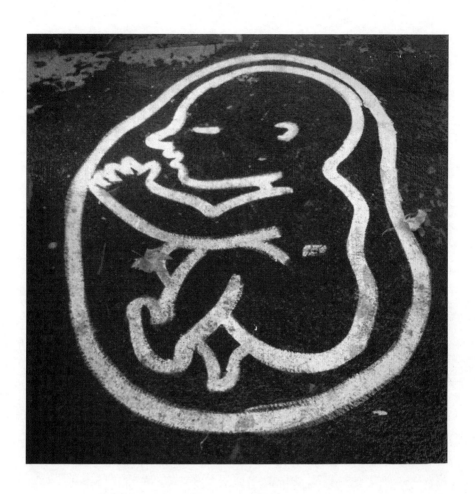

SEPTEMBER 1, 2012 – PARIS, FRANCE

The first picture taken in Paris. Immediately after eagerly exiting the Gare du Norde railway station, I kept encountering these images painted all over the streets. As I walked for several blocks they just kept appearing along my path. I didn't think too much of them at the time since my razor sharp focus was on finding my hotel. It wasn't until the next day when once again I found myself rendezvousing with these lima bean shaped paintings all over the Parisian streets that it finally hit me, "It's a fetus!" The very first image I photographed in the city I claimed to mark my new life was also the very symbol of new life itself. If there was ever any doubt in my mind that this whole experience was not divinely orchestrated, the proof that it had been, was perfectly drawn out beneath my feet.

SEPTEMBER 1, 2012

We are all perfect imperfections.

Travel is rarely about time or money. It's mainly about garnering up the courage to sacrifice all that impedes your wanderlust.

Set the village of a turbulent past ablaze. Leave only with the bag of lessons learned strapped on your back and run into the future as fast as you can. Never, never look back.

The truth is none of us know when we will die, yet a great majority of us live as if we are going to exist forever. We wait for the right moment to travel, to leave the things that make us unhappy behind, to fall in love with someone, and to truly feel what it is like to be alive as an adult.

Sadly most of us will never live out our dreams because of this thinking process. We surrender to fear and cowardly justify it by saying that now is not the right time, when in the undistorted reality *now* is the only time we will ever really have.

Lift the embargo, renounce the blockade. The treaty is yours to make. Sign the deal to open the borders of your soul and allow all that the universe has to offer into your realm. Erase your borderlines and implode your Ego's checkpoints. Let cosmic goodness flow through all that is you.

I was once a prisoner sentenced to a life of conventional living and thought. The shackles of society weighed heavy on my feet. Seldom absent, other people's ways of thinking on how I should live were always the first to answer my waking roll call. Every morning I scratched a line on the walls of my cell to mark a day of my life lost trying to please someone else, or to fit in.

Dead on my feet from all the crap being shoved down my throat, I said screw you to "normalcy", no longer did I want to be accepted. I just wanted to be happy! I did what all my heroes from the past had done. I broke free and I ran far, far away from mass thinking. I also made a vow to build a giant stick of philosophical TNT and return to that old dirty brick house of lies, blow it up, and set everyone in it free. Now my stick of super awesome dynamite is ready to be lit and I'm making my way back to the very place that took so much away from me. I'm ready to make its walls crumble. Someone please hand me a match.

SEPTEMBER 2, 2012 – ARCH DE TRIOMPHE

At no time has the future shined, any brighter. The sword of truth I used to slay the demons of the past has never been sharper. I find myself submerged in the waters of peace knowing that I toiled all my battles in great solitude. I've encountered a grander serenity in also understanding that although I wanted to run like a coward toward home or even claim defeat and seek comfort in the arms of another, not in any way, did I wave the white flag. I painstakingly stood there in the complete insanity that lived within me and exorcised it. I silenced the voices.

No matter how far away from home I was or how alone I felt, I grappled my solitary sword and fiercely swung away at every single demon until they ceased to exist. I annihilated everything that was trying to "annihilate" me.

Today I grasp this metaphorical bloody sword with a trembling hand, and I stand here claiming victory. The very monument erected in honor of those who fought for France becomes the symbol of my fight for life. I am triumphant. I know that there will be more battles ahead but I fear not of what's to come because I've never felt this powerful; never have I been this wise.

There is an insurmountable amount of freedom found when you realize that all you have within is all that you really need.

September 3, 2012 – The Eiffel Tower

The Eiffel Tower was widely critiqued, considered an eyesore by many, and even thought impossible to build. Now one cannot think of France without it coming to mind. It is a symbol of a nation, a timeless captivator of imaginations from all walks of life. This beacon of hope serves as testament that when one dreams with all their might and goes against popular belief to achieve this dream, one is capable of transforming the collective human psyche.

Dwarfed at the feet of this immovable iron treasure, I poured these words onto paper: "To all the dreamers, the believers, the doers, know that there will come a moment in your existence when you will cross the threshold between what is fantasy and reality. There will be an instant when you're living life exactly how you always dreamt it to be. It's all but a matter of having a resilient belief in self and passing the tests of your faith. Not for one second do you give up, never squander hope and most importantly do not lose sight of the existence of a higher power. Believe in the gracious hand of the Universe, reach for it, as it will elevate you to places grander than life itself. Be confident in knowing that you too can build your very own Tower."

Not a single penny is needed to drift into a dream. All you have to do is close your eyes and let your mind take you to that effervescent place that is all yours.

The need to be always right, to be first, to prove something, to make it a point, to obtain things to say that we did or can are all acts of our unattended, unchecked egos trying to secure its existence in the world outside of our minds. It is the very ego that is killing our environment, our relationships, our rich traditions and cultures. It is that same sick and delusional thinking process that has murdered millions of people throughout human history. If the ego continues to live as rampant as it does it will eventually kill us all. We need to stop it all costs. The very first step is to consciously be aware of it from deeply within.

Louvre Museum

To say that the treasure troves of the art world are stored here is an understatement. With 360,000 pieces in its 650,000 square feet, this grand palace feels more like a megamall than a museum. It is head-spinning and impossible to fully explore in just one visit. Like most first timers I grabbed a handy map and searched for the room where its most famous resident resides: The *Mona Lisa*. I noticed that she's not immediately accessible and decided to take my chances in finding her by purposelessly strolling. In doing so I found myself flipping through the pages of a living art history book. One moment I was encircled by the monuments of ancient Egypt's splendor and another I was begging to be held in the arms of Venus de Milo. Where did they go anyway?

I was thrilled by how quickly I was teleported from one time period to another and zealously dashed from grand hall to grand hall like a contestant on Supermarket Sweep. "Ooh look at that... and that," I repeatedly said to myself. The fervor was periodically paused by jaw-dropping masterpieces. My favorite: *Le Sacre de Napoléon* (The Coronation of Napoleon) by Jacques-Louis David. Larger than life, painted with such precision and mastery I could not help but feel like I was partaking in the tiny emperor's crowning. I imagined the whole of France on that day; proud.

Thirty minutes later I had reached the *Mona Lisa*. She was confined by a velvet rope with brawny security guards on both sides. The look on their faces said: *Cross this rope and you'll get tackled.* Skirting the blockade were flocks of crazed spectators all vying for a spot to snap a perfect picture. Polite shoves and indiscreet elbowing was fair game.

It was finally my turn to come face to canvas with Leonardo Davinci's work of genius. The miniature size caught me by surprise. I gazed in wonderment for 10 seconds before I felt a not so polite shove. I was fine with moving. I had experienced my moment, my date with the *Mona Lisa* was over.

Never be complacent with a life of mediocrity or smallness. Always seek to live a life of splendid grandeur. Make every moment a *Mona Lisa* one.

SEPTEMBER 4, 2012

The most beautiful thing about life is that it's never too late to start all over again.

A complete renaissance of human consciousness is well underway. Humanity has hit a plateau. We've realized that mindless consumption and glorification of material goods and possessions leads to an empty and unfulfilled life. We've begun to ask who we are when we strip ourselves of our titles, jobs, cars, houses and social status. Realizing that when we pose this question we understand that we all are the same, we are all one. We all deserve the same treatment, the same love and compassion, same healthcare, same access to clean water, food, freedom; the list is endless. The days of self-centered living are scantly numbered.

If you are experiencing a newfound interest in spirituality, or are pondering similar things as I've written about, fear not following your heart. Talk openly about your experiences with others. You're not alone. Your contribution to this awakening is a fundamental step for humankind to ensure its continued existence; the Spiritual Revolution is very much in full bloom.

A moment of weakness is a tremendous opportunity to draw and gain strength.

Positive thinking and beliefs will only offer an endless world of miracles and wonder.

Light the world with your smile and torch the path of your life with absolute passion. Be fearless with your heart and surrender it to love every single time it knocks on your door. Take monumental risks, dream far and wide.

The harder one works on the spiritual realm the easier the physical one eventually becomes.

Today I've had the self-realization on the fact that I took a gargantuan leap of faith and landed directly on my feet. Divinity has always been present.

If you don't want to wake up with regret one day wishing you would have followed your heart's desires then make sure to get up every morning and take one small step toward that dream or goal. Ask for help from The Divine through prayer. Fiercely hold on to the thought that infinite persistency is the key to attainment. Look for the "signs". This and only this way will you eventually manifest all that your heart desires and embody the person you wish to become.

Although it can't be recorded or even heard there is a sonic boom type of vibration behind every positive thought that is highly capable of muting even the loudest of negative minds.

It is only natural that if you practice sharing good things, speak only of those good things and act in a good and wholesome way that good will become the predominant contributor of your life's events.

ORLY INTERNATIONAL AIRPORT PARIS, FRANCE

For many years I spent most of my time foolishly pawning my thoughts on the philosophies that went something like: "If I won the lottery, if had a better job, if this, if that, if things were only different than what I had, then I could really be happy." I lived in this phantom town where my life was perfect depending on an outside source or condition, and the future was the only place where it could manifest. The now was never good enough. I was basically ready for a white jacket and a van to the psychic ward. It wasn't till that singular waking moment when I decided that I need not wait to win the lottery, have a nicer office or whatever other buffoonery I allowed myself to believe in, was when everything transformed. I realized I had already won the biggest prize in the universe, that I was the tycoon-of-tycoons by owning health and life. The only 'if', was that if I was really going to make my dreams a reality I needed to do so in the very now by tuning in to the unequivocal strength that can be drawn from having faith in Spirit.

Having more confidence in myself and in the gracious hand of Source, I worked and prayed a lot harder. I made inconceivable sacrifices by giving up almost all that I owned. I evicted the antiquated thoughts of doubt and disbelief from the palatial estate they had built in my mind and replaced them with the secure tenants of belief in self and faith in a higher power. I became a lot less frivolous with my time and utilized all of my waking hours wisely toward my goals. I practiced affirmations both verbally and in writing while constantly praising Spirit. I emulated those I admired. I began to speak and write like the person I so badly desired to become, and in doing so I became him.

I endured every "gauntlet" The Universe threw at me, knowing that I would survive. Never did I ever complain because I found that whining is the absolute most counterproductive behavior a healthy human being living a privileged lifestyle can indulge in. Lest we forget our invalid, sick, famished, dirt poor and blind human brothers and sisters who live an unjust sufferance and say not enough about their troubles. Do not complain.

Ceaselessly chase all your dreams with a pure heart and conviction, believe in miracles, follow the "signs", waste not a fraction of a fraction of a thought on what others think (it's useless). Do this with the understanding that The Divine, the Universe, God, Spirit, Source or whatever you wish to call your higher power will only hand you what can tackle, and your desires will manifest.

Manifest, manifest, manifest.

My biggest sense of achievement from this journey comes not from gazing at the great Pyramids of Giza, the Sydney Opera House or the Hagia Sofia. It's extrapolated from a powerful discovery about humanity that I've made. This discovery of which this series of photos proves is the following: Open yourself up to the world and the world will open itself up to you. Do not judge others and others will not judge you.

THANK YOU WORLD BECAUSE OF YOU I HAVE BECOME A BETTER MAN!

In chronological order from top left:

- Village Girls at the Sabeto Mudsprings in the Fiji Islands.
- Monk at the Temples of Angkor Wat in Siem Reap, Cambodia.
- My Greek family in their home in Athens, Greece.
- My Egyptian family at the Saladin Citadel in Cairo, Egypt.

ABOUT THE AUTHOR

Hector Jesus Arencibia is a first generation American. He was born and raised in Miami, Florida, and is the son of two Cuban Immigrants. He currently resides in Miami and has seized the opportune moments to live in magical cities such as Vienna, Los Angeles, Budapest and New York City, which have all heavily influenced the person he is today. He has traveled extensively around the world having set foot on the soil of six of the seven continents, and has visited major spiritual sites such as: Jerusalem, Machu Picchu, the Acropolis, Palenque, Mount Shasta, Petra, Stonehenge, The Pyramids of Giza, and The Temples of Angkor Wat to name a few.

Made in the USA
San Bernardino, CA
31 December 2017